Zero Trust and Privilege in IAM

James Relington

DEDICATION

To my family, whose support and encouragement have been my greatest motivation. To my colleagues and mentors, who have generously shared their knowledge and experience. And to all those passionate about technology and security, who strive to build a safer digital world.

ACKNOWLEDGEMENTS

I would like to express my gratitude to everyone who contributed to the creation of this book. To my family and friends for their unwavering support, to my colleagues and mentors for their valuable contributions, and to the technology community for continually sharing knowledge and pushing the boundaries of innovation. A special thank you to those who reviewed, provided feedback, and inspired me along this journey. Their encouragement and experience have made this work possible.

Introduction to Identity and Access Management (IAM)

Identity and Access Management (IAM) is a critical discipline in modern cybersecurity, enabling organizations to manage digital identities and control access to resources in a secure and efficient manner. As businesses increasingly move to cloud environments, adopt remote work models, and integrate third-party services, the need for a robust IAM framework has never been more essential. IAM serves as the foundation of security policies, ensuring that only authorized users have access to the right data, systems, and applications at the right time, minimizing the risk of data breaches and insider threats.

IAM is built upon the fundamental principle of identity, which refers to the unique representation of an entity within a system. This entity can be a human user, an application, or even an automated process. Managing these identities involves assigning credentials, such as usernames and passwords, as well as implementing authentication mechanisms to verify legitimacy. Traditionally, access control relied on perimeter-based security models, where organizations assumed that everything inside the corporate network was trustworthy. However, as cyber threats have evolved and network boundaries have become more fluid, this approach has proven insufficient. IAM has shifted towards a more dynamic, identity-centric model that aligns with the principles of Zero Trust, where no user or device is inherently trusted by default.

A key aspect of IAM is authentication, the process of verifying an identity before granting access to a system. Simple password-based authentication methods are no longer sufficient, as attackers have become adept at credential theft and phishing attacks. Organizations now rely on Multi-Factor Authentication (MFA) to enhance security, requiring users to provide additional verification factors such as biometrics, one-time passcodes, or security keys. Strong authentication ensures that even if a password is compromised, an attacker cannot easily gain access to sensitive systems. However, authentication alone is not enough; access control mechanisms must also be in place to ensure that authenticated users can only access resources that align with their role and responsibilities.

Authorization is another fundamental component of IAM, determining what actions an authenticated user is permitted to perform. Organizations implement various access control models, including Role-Based Access Control (RBAC) and Attribute-Based Access Control (ABAC), to enforce security policies. RBAC assigns access permissions based on predefined roles, ensuring that users can only interact with systems in ways relevant to their job functions. ABAC, on the other hand, considers dynamic attributes such as user location, device security posture, or time of access to make more granular access decisions. These models prevent excessive privileges, a common security risk where users retain unnecessary access to systems long after their responsibilities have changed.

The lifecycle of an identity within an IAM system involves multiple stages, starting with identity creation and onboarding. When a new user joins an organization, IAM processes establish their digital identity, assign appropriate access rights, and ensure compliance with security policies. Throughout an employee's tenure, their access needs may evolve as they move between roles or departments. IAM solutions enable automated provisioning and de-provisioning of access rights, reducing the risk of orphaned accounts—accounts that remain active even after an employee has left the organization. This automation not only improves security but also enhances operational efficiency by eliminating the manual processes traditionally associated with user access management.

Identity Governance and Administration (IGA) is a subset of IAM that focuses on compliance, auditing, and policy enforcement. Regulatory frameworks such as GDPR, HIPAA, and SOX require organizations to maintain strict controls over identity and access management. IGA solutions provide visibility into user access patterns, detect anomalies, and enforce policies that align with regulatory requirements. Periodic access reviews ensure that only the necessary individuals retain access to critical systems, reducing the risk of insider threats and accidental data exposure.

IAM extends beyond human identities to include machine identities, which encompass service accounts, APIs, and automated processes. As organizations embrace cloud computing and DevOps methodologies, the number of machine identities has grown exponentially. Securing these identities is just as important as managing human access, as attackers often exploit improperly secured service accounts to move laterally within a network. Implementing strong authentication, enforcing least privilege access, and continuously monitoring machine identities are essential strategies for mitigating security risks.

IAM solutions integrate with a wide range of enterprise applications, including cloud platforms, customer relationship management (CRM) systems, and enterprise resource planning (ERP) software. Many organizations leverage Single Sign-On (SSO) solutions to streamline user authentication across multiple applications, reducing password fatigue and improving user experience. Federated identity management allows users to authenticate once and access multiple services across different organizations without needing separate credentials. This interoperability is particularly important in hybrid and multi-cloud environments where seamless access to resources is necessary for operational efficiency.

The growing adoption of Zero Trust principles has further reshaped IAM strategies. Zero Trust operates under the assumption that threats exist both inside and outside an organization's network, requiring continuous verification of user identities and device security before granting access. This approach aligns with the principle of least privilege, ensuring that users only have the minimum level of access required to perform their tasks. Continuous authentication mechanisms, behavioral analytics, and real-time risk assessments are increasingly integrated into IAM solutions to enhance security while maintaining usability.

As cyber threats become more sophisticated, IAM is evolving to incorporate artificial intelligence (AI) and machine learning (ML) to improve identity verification and threat detection. AI-powered analytics help identify unusual access patterns, detect compromised accounts, and automate response actions to mitigate risks. The combination of traditional IAM practices with AI-driven insights enhances an organization's ability to prevent unauthorized access and respond to security incidents in real time.

Effective IAM implementation requires a balance between security and user experience. Overly restrictive access controls can hinder productivity, while lax security measures expose organizations to risks. Organizations must adopt a risk-based approach to IAM, ensuring that security measures are proportionate to the sensitivity of the data and applications being protected. Continuous monitoring, policy enforcement, and user education play a crucial role in maintaining an effective IAM framework.

Identity and Access Management is no longer just a security function—it is a business enabler that supports digital transformation, regulatory compliance, and operational efficiency. Organizations that invest in a robust IAM strategy can protect their digital assets, improve user experience, and build a strong security foundation that adapts to the evolving cyber threat landscape. As the technological ecosystem continues to expand, IAM will remain a cornerstone of modern cybersecurity, ensuring that organizations can securely manage identities and access in an increasingly complex digital world.

The Evolution of Cybersecurity: From Perimeter to Zero Trust

Cybersecurity has undergone a profound transformation over the past several decades, adapting to an ever-changing threat landscape and shifting technological paradigms. In the early days of digital security, organizations relied heavily on a perimeter-based defense model, assuming that threats originated from outside their network while internal systems remained inherently trustworthy. This approach, often referred to as the "castle-and-moat" strategy, centered on firewalls, intrusion detection systems, and network segmentation to keep unauthorized entities at bay. While effective in a time when corporate infrastructure was largely confined to on-premises data centers and controlled networks, this model began to falter as business operations expanded beyond traditional boundaries.

The emergence of the internet, remote work, cloud computing, and mobile technology fundamentally altered the security equation. Perimeter defenses became increasingly inadequate as users, applications, and data moved outside corporate walls. Organizations began relying on virtual private networks (VPNs) to provide secure remote access to employees and contractors, but these solutions introduced their own vulnerabilities. A compromised VPN credential could grant an attacker unrestricted access to internal resources, undermining the security perimeter altogether. The rise of bring-your-own-device (BYOD) policies further complicated security management, as personal laptops, smartphones, and tablets connected to corporate networks, often without the same level of protection as managed devices.

Cyber threats evolved in parallel with these changes, growing in sophistication and targeting organizations through multiple attack vectors. Traditional perimeter defenses, designed to filter out known threats, struggled to detect novel malware, zero-day exploits, and advanced persistent threats (APTs). Phishing attacks became a primary method for cybercriminals to steal credentials, bypassing firewalls and security filters by exploiting human behavior. Once an attacker gained access to an internal network, lateral movement techniques allowed them to navigate through systems undetected, escalating privileges and exfiltrating sensitive data. The increasing frequency and severity of data breaches made it clear that a new security paradigm was necessary.

The concept of Zero Trust emerged as a response to the limitations of perimeter-based security. Unlike traditional models that assumed internal trust, Zero Trust operates on the principle that trust should never be implicit, regardless of whether a user or device is inside or outside the corporate network. This approach mandates continuous verification of identities, strict access controls, and the principle of least privilege, ensuring that users and systems only have access to the resources they absolutely need. Instead of relying on a single security perimeter, Zero Trust enforces security policies at multiple levels, applying authentication, encryption, and behavioral analysis at every stage of access.

One of the core tenets of Zero Trust is identity-centric security. Since traditional network boundaries are no longer reliable, verifying the identity of users, devices, and applications becomes the primary means of securing access. Multi-Factor Authentication (MFA) plays a crucial role in strengthening identity verification, reducing the risk of unauthorized access due to stolen passwords. Beyond authentication, Zero Trust continuously evaluates risk throughout a user's session, taking into account contextual factors such as device health, geographic location, and behavioral patterns. If an anomaly is detected—such as a login attempt from an unfamiliar location or an unpatched device—the system can prompt for additional verification or restrict access entirely.

Another key aspect of Zero Trust is micro-segmentation, which divides networks into isolated segments to limit the spread of potential attacks. In traditional environments, once an attacker breaches the network perimeter, they often have unfettered access to multiple systems. Micro-segmentation mitigates this risk by enforcing strict access controls between different network segments, ensuring that even if an attacker gains access to one system, they cannot move laterally to others without authentication. This strategy is particularly important in cloud environments, where workloads and applications are distributed across multiple platforms and services.

Zero Trust also incorporates continuous monitoring and behavioral analytics to detect and respond to threats in real time. Traditional security models often relied on periodic access reviews and rule-based alerts, which could fail to catch sophisticated attacks in progress. By leveraging artificial intelligence and machine learning, Zero Trust solutions can analyze user behavior and detect deviations from normal patterns, identifying potential threats before they escalate. This proactive approach shifts cybersecurity from a reactive stance—responding to incidents after they occur—to a preventive one, mitigating risks before they can cause harm.

As organizations adopt cloud-first strategies, the importance of Zero Trust becomes even more evident. Cloud environments are inherently dynamic, with users accessing resources from multiple locations and devices. Unlike on-premises systems that can be protected by a well-defined security perimeter, cloud applications and data must be secured through identity-based controls and continuous access evaluation. Many cloud service providers have embraced Zero Trust principles, offering identity and access management (IAM) solutions that integrate with security frameworks to enforce least privilege access and prevent unauthorized activity.

Regulatory and compliance requirements have also accelerated the adoption of Zero Trust. Organizations across industries must adhere to strict security standards to protect sensitive data and maintain compliance with regulations such as GDPR, HIPAA, and NIST. Traditional security models often struggled to meet these requirements, as they relied on implicit trust within internal networks. Zero Trust provides a more robust framework for achieving compliance, ensuring that access to data and systems is continuously monitored, restricted based on risk levels, and auditable for security governance purposes.

The transition from perimeter-based security to Zero Trust is not without challenges. Organizations must rethink their existing security architectures, invest in modern IAM solutions, and implement new access policies that align with Zero Trust principles. This shift requires collaboration across IT, security, and business teams to ensure that security measures do not hinder productivity. While Zero Trust enhances security, it must also provide a seamless user experience, balancing strong authentication mechanisms with accessibility and efficiency.

As cyber threats continue to evolve, Zero Trust represents the next phase in the ongoing evolution of cybersecurity. By eliminating implicit trust, enforcing continuous verification, and implementing granular access controls, Zero Trust provides organizations with a resilient and adaptable security framework. This paradigm shift is essential in a world where digital transformation, remote work, and cloud adoption have redefined the way organizations operate and interact with technology. Embracing Zero Trust is not merely a security enhancement but a fundamental necessity for protecting modern enterprises against increasingly sophisticated threats.

Defining Zero Trust in IAM

Zero Trust is a security framework that fundamentally redefines the way organizations approach identity and access management (IAM). Traditional security models relied on the assumption that entities inside a corporate network were inherently trustworthy while external entities posed a threat. This perimeter-based security approach was effective when organizations operated within controlled environments, where all resources and users were confined to an internal network. However, the rise of cloud computing, mobile workforces, and sophisticated cyber threats has rendered this model obsolete. Zero Trust shifts the focus from network location to identity verification, enforcing strict access controls and continuous validation of trust at every step.

At its core, Zero Trust operates under the principle of "never trust, always verify." This means that no user, device, or application is granted access based on assumed trust, even if it originates from within the organization's infrastructure. Every request for access is treated as potentially malicious until verified through authentication, contextual risk analysis, and policy enforcement. IAM plays a crucial role in enabling this framework by ensuring that identities are properly authenticated, authorized, and continuously monitored to prevent unauthorized access.

Authentication is the first pillar of Zero Trust in IAM, requiring users to prove their identities before being granted access to resources. Password-based authentication alone is no longer sufficient due to the widespread threats of credential theft, phishing, and brute-force attacks. Organizations implementing Zero Trust adopt Multi-Factor Authentication (MFA) to add an additional layer of security. MFA requires users to provide two or more factors of verification, such as a password combined with biometric authentication, a one-time passcode, or a security token. Even if an attacker obtains a user's password, the additional authentication factors make unauthorized access significantly more difficult.

Beyond authentication, Zero Trust enforces strict authorization controls based on the principle of least privilege. Users are granted only the minimum permissions necessary to perform their job functions, reducing the risk of excessive access. Traditional access control models, such as Role-Based Access Control (RBAC), assign permissions based on predefined roles, ensuring that employees only have access to relevant resources. More advanced models, like Attribute-Based Access Control (ABAC), refine access permissions based on contextual factors, such as location, device security posture, and time of access. These granular access controls prevent privilege escalation attacks and unauthorized data exposure.

Continuous monitoring and adaptive access control are essential components of Zero Trust in IAM. Unlike traditional models that perform authentication at the beginning of a session and assume trust throughout, Zero Trust continuously evaluates user behavior, risk levels, and environmental conditions. Identity analytics and behavioral analytics play a key role in detecting anomalies that may indicate compromised credentials or insider threats. If a user suddenly accesses sensitive data from an unfamiliar device or location, the system can trigger additional authentication challenges or revoke access entirely. This real-time assessment ensures that trust is not static but dynamically adjusted based on risk.

Zero Trust also emphasizes the security of machine identities, which include service accounts, APIs, and automated processes. As organizations adopt cloud computing and automation, the number of machine identities has grown exponentially, presenting new attack surfaces. Traditional IAM systems focused primarily on human identities, but Zero Trust extends security principles to non-human entities as well. Secure API authentication, workload identity verification, and Just-In-Time (JIT) access provisioning ensure that machine identities do not become weak links in the security chain. Implementing strict identity governance for machine-to-machine interactions prevents unauthorized access and minimizes the risk of supply chain attacks.

Network segmentation and micro-segmentation are additional layers of Zero Trust that work in tandem with IAM. Traditionally, once a user gained access to a corporate network, they could move laterally across different systems with minimal restrictions. This lack of segmentation has led to devastating breaches, where attackers exploit a single compromised account to navigate through an entire IT environment. Zero Trust mitigates this risk by enforcing micro-segmentation, isolating resources based on sensitivity and function. Even if an attacker compromises one system, they cannot access other critical assets without undergoing additional authentication and authorization checks.

Cloud environments have accelerated the adoption of Zero Trust in IAM, as traditional network perimeters no longer apply to distributed infrastructures. Organizations leverage Identity-as-a-Service (IDaaS) platforms to implement Zero Trust principles across cloud applications, ensuring that user identities are centrally managed and protected. Federated identity management enables seamless authentication across different cloud providers while maintaining strict security controls. Organizations also implement Continuous Access Evaluation (CAE), where access permissions are dynamically reassessed based on changing risk conditions, such as device security posture or user behavior anomalies.

Zero Trust IAM is also vital for securing remote workforces. With employees accessing corporate resources from various locations and personal devices, organizations cannot rely on traditional network-based security. Implementing a Zero Trust framework ensures that access requests undergo rigorous authentication and authorization checks, regardless of where the request originates. Endpoint security, device trust verification, and risk-based authentication further strengthen security by ensuring that only compliant devices and verified identities can access critical systems.

Compliance and regulatory frameworks align closely with Zero Trust IAM principles. Regulations such as GDPR, HIPAA, and NIST mandate strict access controls, identity governance, and data protection measures. Zero Trust provides organizations with a structured approach to meeting compliance requirements by enforcing least privilege access, continuous monitoring, and audit logging. By implementing Zero Trust IAM, organizations can improve their security posture while simultaneously achieving regulatory compliance.

The adoption of artificial intelligence and machine learning enhances the effectiveness of Zero Trust in IAM by enabling advanced threat detection and response. AI-driven identity analytics help identify patterns of abnormal behavior, detect compromised accounts, and trigger automated security responses. Machine learning models can assess risk scores in real time, adjusting authentication and access policies dynamically. These intelligent capabilities ensure that Zero Trust remains adaptive and capable of responding to emerging threats without relying solely on predefined security rules.

Organizations implementing Zero Trust in IAM must balance security with user experience. Overly restrictive authentication and access policies can frustrate users and hinder productivity, leading to potential workarounds that introduce security risks. Zero Trust IAM solutions must be designed to provide frictionless authentication while maintaining high security standards. Passwordless authentication, biometric verification, and single sign-on (SSO) solutions help streamline access without compromising security.

Zero Trust in IAM represents a paradigm shift in cybersecurity, replacing outdated perimeter-based defenses with identity-centric security models. By enforcing continuous verification, least privilege access, and adaptive risk-based authentication, organizations can significantly reduce the risk of data breaches and insider threats. As digital transformation accelerates and cyber threats become more sophisticated, Zero Trust IAM will continue to be a foundational security framework, ensuring that trust is never assumed but always verified.

The Principles of Least Privilege Access

The principle of least privilege (PoLP) is a fundamental security concept that limits users, applications, and systems to the minimum level of access required to perform their functions. This approach minimizes the risk of unauthorized access, data breaches, and insider threats by restricting unnecessary permissions that could be exploited by attackers. Least privilege is a core component of identity and access management (IAM), ensuring that users and systems operate within well-defined security boundaries. By applying this principle, organizations reduce their attack surface, improve compliance, and strengthen overall security posture.

Access control in traditional IT environments often relied on broad permissions, granting users excessive privileges that extended beyond their job responsibilities. This outdated practice increased the likelihood of privilege abuse, either through malicious intent or accidental misuse. Employees with elevated access rights could unintentionally expose sensitive data, install unauthorized applications, or make critical system changes that led to security vulnerabilities. Attackers targeting such accounts could escalate their privileges and gain full control over an organization's infrastructure. The least privilege model mitigates these risks by enforcing strict access policies, ensuring that users and applications only have the permissions they genuinely need.

One of the primary implementations of least privilege is Role-Based

Access Control (RBAC), where access is granted based on predefined roles associated with specific job functions. By assigning users to roles with clearly defined permissions, organizations can prevent excessive access rights and maintain consistency in security policies. For example, a junior accountant may only have access to financial records necessary for their daily tasks, while a senior manager might have broader access to financial reports but still lack administrative privileges. RBAC simplifies access management, reducing the complexity of manually assigning permissions while maintaining control over who can access sensitive resources.

Attribute-Based Access Control (ABAC) enhances the least privilege model by adding contextual factors to access decisions. Unlike RBAC, which relies on static roles, ABAC considers attributes such as user location, device security posture, and time of access. A financial analyst working in the office may be allowed to access confidential reports, but if they attempt to access the same reports from an untrusted device outside corporate networks, their access might be denied or require additional authentication. ABAC provides dynamic and granular control over access rights, reducing unnecessary exposure to sensitive data while allowing flexibility in legitimate use cases.

Just-In-Time (JIT) access is another critical aspect of enforcing least privilege. Instead of granting permanent elevated access, JIT access provisions privileges only for a limited duration when needed. This method is especially useful for administrators, developers, and support teams who occasionally require high-level permissions to troubleshoot or configure systems. By ensuring that privileged access is temporary and tightly controlled, JIT access prevents accounts from retaining excessive permissions long after they are needed, significantly reducing the risk of misuse or compromise.

Privileged Access Management (PAM) plays a crucial role in implementing least privilege by securing and monitoring privileged accounts. Administrative accounts, service accounts, and system-level users often have elevated privileges that, if compromised, could lead to catastrophic security breaches. PAM solutions enforce least privilege by requiring users to request access through a controlled workflow, with approval processes, logging, and session monitoring in place. This ensures that privileged access is granted only when necessary and that every action taken by a privileged user is recorded for audit purposes. PAM solutions also rotate and vault privileged credentials, preventing unauthorized use of static passwords that attackers could exploit.

The principle of least privilege is not limited to human users; it also applies to machine identities, including service accounts, APIs, and automated processes. Many organizations overlook the security of machine identities, often assigning excessive permissions to service accounts that interact with databases, cloud applications, and critical infrastructure. Attackers frequently exploit overprivileged machine accounts to move laterally within a network and escalate privileges. By enforcing least privilege for machine identities, organizations can restrict API access, implement token-based authentication, and ensure that automated processes operate with minimal necessary permissions.

Endpoint security is another area where least privilege access is essential. Many cyberattacks originate from compromised endpoints, where malware exploits users' elevated privileges to gain control over systems. Enforcing least privilege on endpoints ensures that users do not have administrative rights that could allow malware to install itself, disable security controls, or execute unauthorized actions. Organizations implement endpoint privilege management solutions to restrict administrative access while allowing necessary software installations through approval workflows. By reducing endpoint privileges, organizations can limit the impact of malware infections and unauthorized system changes.

Cloud environments present unique challenges in enforcing least privilege due to their dynamic nature and extensive use of cloud services. Many organizations struggle with excessive permissions granted to cloud users, leading to security misconfigurations that expose sensitive data. Cloud IAM policies must be carefully designed to ensure that users, applications, and workloads have the minimum necessary permissions to perform their functions. Cloud providers offer tools such as identity federation, conditional access policies, and access reviews to help organizations enforce least privilege across cloud environments. Implementing least privilege in the cloud requires continuous monitoring of access permissions, identifying overly permissive roles, and revoking unnecessary privileges.

Auditing and monitoring are critical to maintaining a least privilege model. Organizations must continuously review access rights, detect privilege escalation attempts, and analyze user behavior for anomalies. Automated access reviews help identify unused or excessive privileges, allowing security teams to adjust permissions accordingly. By integrating IAM with security information and event management (SIEM) solutions, organizations can gain real-time insights into access patterns and respond to suspicious activity. Continuous enforcement of least privilege requires proactive monitoring, automated remediation, and regular policy updates to adapt to evolving security threats.

Balancing security and usability is a challenge in implementing least privilege. Overly restrictive access controls can hinder productivity, leading users to seek workarounds that introduce new security risks. Organizations must design least privilege policies that align with business needs while maintaining strong security controls. Implementing single sign-on (SSO), adaptive authentication, and user-friendly access request workflows can improve security without compromising efficiency. By incorporating least privilege into the overall IAM strategy, organizations can achieve a balance between robust security and seamless user experience.

Least privilege is a foundational security principle that enhances protection against unauthorized access, insider threats, and privilege abuse. By enforcing strict access controls, adopting role-based and attribute-based policies, implementing privileged access management, and continuously monitoring permissions, organizations can significantly reduce their risk exposure. As cyber threats evolve, the adoption of least privilege across human and machine identities, cloud environments, and endpoints remains a critical strategy in safeguarding sensitive data and maintaining a resilient security posture.

Zero Trust Architecture: Key Components

Zero Trust Architecture (ZTA) is a cybersecurity framework that assumes no entity, whether inside or outside an organization's network, should be trusted by default. Instead of relying on a traditional perimeter-based security model, Zero Trust continuously verifies identity, enforces strict access controls, and applies security policies dynamically based on real-time risk assessments. This approach is designed to prevent unauthorized access, minimize attack surfaces, and reduce the impact of potential security breaches. Implementing Zero Trust Architecture requires the integration of several key components that work together to create a resilient security model.

Identity and Access Management (IAM) is at the core of Zero Trust, ensuring that all users, devices, and applications are authenticated before accessing resources. Strong authentication mechanisms, such as Multi-Factor Authentication (MFA), help verify user identities and prevent credential-based attacks. Traditional username and password combinations are no longer sufficient, as attackers frequently use phishing, brute-force attacks, and credential stuffing to gain unauthorized access. Zero Trust enforces strict authentication policies, requiring multiple verification factors, such as biometrics, security keys, or one-time passcodes, before granting access. In addition to authentication, IAM ensures that users are only authorized to access resources that align with their role, following the principle of least privilege.

Micro-segmentation is another fundamental component of Zero Trust, designed to limit lateral movement within a network. In traditional security models, once an attacker gains access to a corporate network, they can move freely between systems with minimal restrictions. Zero Trust mitigates this risk by dividing networks into smaller, isolated segments, each protected with its own access controls. This ensures that even if a system is compromised, the attacker cannot easily access other sensitive resources. Micro-segmentation is particularly important in cloud environments and hybrid infrastructures, where workloads and applications are distributed across multiple data centers and cloud providers. By implementing micro-segmentation, organizations can enforce granular security policies, restricting access based on identity, device posture, and application behavior.

Continuous monitoring and threat detection are essential for maintaining Zero Trust security. Unlike traditional security models that verify access at the initial login stage, Zero Trust continuously evaluates user behavior, access patterns, and contextual risk factors throughout a session. Security Information and Event Management (SIEM) systems and User and Entity Behavior Analytics (UEBA) solutions help detect anomalies that may indicate a security threat. If an authenticated user suddenly exhibits unusual behavior, such as accessing sensitive data from an unfamiliar location or attempting to download large amounts of information, Zero Trust policies can trigger additional authentication challenges or automatically revoke access. By continuously monitoring access and analyzing risk in real time, organizations can prevent unauthorized activities and respond to threats before they escalate.

Endpoint security plays a crucial role in Zero Trust by ensuring that devices accessing corporate resources meet security requirements. Organizations cannot assume that all devices are secure, as employees often use personal laptops, smartphones, and tablets to access work-related applications. Zero Trust requires endpoint verification, assessing whether a device is patched, free of malware, and compliant with security policies before granting access. Device posture checks, such as verifying antivirus status, encryption settings, and software updates, help reduce the risk of compromised endpoints being used as entry points for attackers. If a device fails to meet security requirements, access can be restricted or redirected to a remediation process before being granted permission to sensitive resources.

Zero Trust also incorporates Secure Access Service Edge (SASE), a cloud-based security framework that combines network security functions with Zero Trust principles. SASE enables organizations to enforce security policies regardless of user location, making it ideal for remote workforces and distributed environments. Instead of relying on traditional VPNs, which grant broad network access once authenticated, SASE applies Zero Trust Network Access (ZTNA) principles, ensuring that users can only access the specific applications they are authorized to use. By integrating cloud-delivered security solutions, such as Secure Web Gateways (SWG) and Cloud Access Security Brokers (CASB), SASE enhances Zero Trust by providing comprehensive protection for cloud applications, internet traffic, and remote users.

The implementation of Just-In-Time (JIT) access further strengthens Zero Trust security by limiting the duration of privileged access. Traditional access management models often grant long-term administrative privileges, increasing the risk of privilege misuse and insider threats. JIT access ensures that users and applications receive elevated privileges only for a short period, reducing the potential attack surface. Once the task is completed, the elevated access is automatically revoked, minimizing the risk of unauthorized actions. JIT access is particularly valuable for system administrators, DevOps engineers, and third-party contractors who require temporary access to critical systems without maintaining persistent privileges.

Data security is another critical component of Zero Trust, focusing on protecting sensitive information at rest, in transit, and during processing. Encryption plays a vital role in securing data, ensuring that unauthorized users cannot access or manipulate information even if they gain access to a system. Zero Trust enforces strict data access policies, classifying data based on sensitivity and applying appropriate controls. Data Loss Prevention (DLP) solutions help prevent accidental or intentional data leaks by monitoring and restricting unauthorized data transfers. Organizations also implement digital rights management (DRM) and attribute-based encryption to protect intellectual property and confidential business information.

Zero Trust is heavily reliant on automation and orchestration to enforce security policies efficiently. Manual security processes are often slow and prone to errors, making it difficult to respond to threats in real time. Zero Trust frameworks integrate with Security Orchestration, Automation, and Response (SOAR) solutions to automate incident response, threat mitigation, and access control enforcement. Automated identity verification, risk-based authentication, and policy-driven access control help organizations scale Zero Trust implementations while maintaining a consistent security posture. By leveraging artificial intelligence and machine learning, Zero Trust systems can adapt to emerging threats, refining security policies based on evolving attack techniques.

Zero Trust Architecture is a comprehensive security model that replaces outdated perimeter-based defenses with continuous verification, strict access controls, and dynamic security policies. By integrating identity and access management, micro-segmentation, continuous monitoring, endpoint security, and cloud-based security solutions, organizations can create a resilient Zero Trust framework. As cyber threats continue to evolve, Zero Trust provides a scalable and adaptive approach to securing digital assets, ensuring that no user, device, or application is granted trust by default.

IAM in the Modern Enterprise

Identity and Access Management (IAM) is a cornerstone of security and operational efficiency in the modern enterprise. As organizations expand their digital footprints, migrate to cloud environments, and adopt remote work policies, managing identities and access rights has become increasingly complex. IAM is no longer just a security function; it is a strategic necessity that enables businesses to protect sensitive data, maintain regulatory compliance, and streamline user access across multiple systems. A well-implemented IAM framework ensures that employees, contractors, and partners can securely access the resources they need while minimizing the risk of unauthorized access and data breaches.

The traditional enterprise IT landscape consisted of centralized on-premises systems where access controls were relatively straightforward. Employees worked within a controlled environment, accessing applications and data hosted on corporate servers. A perimeter-based security approach was sufficient for protecting internal systems, with firewalls and network-based authentication serving as primary defense mechanisms. However, the shift to cloud computing and software-as-a-service (SaaS) applications has rendered this model obsolete. Employees now require access to a mix of on-premises and cloud-based applications, often from multiple devices and locations. This distributed environment necessitates an identity-centric security model that can verify and authorize users regardless of where they are or what device they are using.

Modern enterprises face the challenge of managing thousands or even millions of digital identities, including human users and machine identities such as service accounts, APIs, and IoT devices. As organizations embrace digital transformation, the number of identity interactions grows exponentially, increasing the risk of unauthorized access and security breaches. IAM solutions provide centralized identity governance, automating user provisioning, enforcing role-based access controls, and integrating with authentication mechanisms to ensure seamless and secure access. By leveraging IAM, enterprises can enforce security policies consistently across hybrid and multi-cloud environments while reducing administrative overhead.

Authentication is a critical aspect of IAM in the modern enterprise. Traditional username and password authentication methods are insufficient in today's threat landscape, as attackers frequently exploit weak passwords, phishing attacks, and credential theft. Organizations are adopting Multi-Factor Authentication (MFA) to add an extra layer of security, requiring users to verify their identity through biometrics, one-time passcodes, or hardware security tokens. Adaptive authentication further enhances security by analyzing contextual factors such as device trust, location, and user behavior to determine whether additional verification is necessary. These measures help mitigate the risk of unauthorized access while maintaining a seamless user experience.

Single Sign-On (SSO) has become a fundamental component of IAM, allowing users to authenticate once and gain access to multiple applications without re-entering credentials. SSO improves security by reducing password fatigue, minimizing the need for users to manage multiple passwords across different systems. Enterprises integrate SSO with cloud identity providers, enabling federated authentication across SaaS applications and external business partners. This approach not only simplifies access management but also strengthens security by centralizing authentication controls and reducing the attack surface associated with password-based authentication.

Privileged Access Management (PAM) is another critical element of IAM in the modern enterprise. Administrators, developers, and executives often require elevated privileges to access sensitive systems and perform critical tasks. However, excessive or uncontrolled privileged access poses a significant security risk, as attackers often target privileged accounts to escalate their access within an organization. PAM solutions enforce least privilege access, ensuring that users only have the permissions necessary to perform their roles. Just-In-Time (JIT) access further enhances security by granting temporary privileges for specific tasks and revoking them once the task is completed. By implementing PAM, enterprises can protect critical assets from insider threats and external attackers.

Identity governance plays a key role in enterprise IAM, ensuring that access rights are assigned appropriately and reviewed regularly. Regulatory frameworks such as GDPR, HIPAA, and SOX mandate strict identity controls, requiring organizations to monitor and audit access to sensitive data. IAM solutions provide automated access reviews, policy enforcement, and real-time monitoring to help enterprises maintain compliance. By continuously evaluating access rights, organizations can prevent privilege creep, where users accumulate unnecessary permissions over time, leading to increased security risks. Identity governance ensures that access policies remain aligned with business needs while minimizing the risk of unauthorized access.

Machine identities are an increasingly important aspect of IAM, as enterprises rely on automation, cloud workloads, and API integrations. Unlike human identities, machine identities do not follow traditional authentication methods, making them a prime target for attackers. Enterprises implement identity-based security controls for service accounts, enforcing authentication and authorization policies to prevent misuse. Secure API authentication mechanisms, such as OAuth and certificate-based authentication, ensure that machine-to-machine interactions remain protected. By managing machine identities with the same level of scrutiny as human identities, organizations can prevent unauthorized access to critical systems and data.

Zero Trust principles have reshaped IAM strategies in the modern enterprise, emphasizing continuous verification and least privilege access. Unlike traditional perimeter-based security models, Zero Trust assumes that no entity—whether inside or outside the network—should be trusted by default. IAM solutions integrate Zero Trust policies by enforcing identity verification at every access request, dynamically adjusting permissions based on risk levels. Continuous authentication, behavioral analytics, and micro-segmentation further enhance security by ensuring that users and devices only access the resources they need at any given time. This approach aligns IAM with modern security challenges, protecting enterprises from evolving cyber threats.

User experience remains a crucial consideration in IAM implementation. Overly complex authentication and access control mechanisms can hinder productivity, leading to frustration among employees and customers. Enterprises must balance security with usability, implementing frictionless authentication solutions such as biometric authentication, passwordless login, and intelligent access workflows. Self-service identity management capabilities empower users to reset passwords, request access, and manage credentials without IT intervention, reducing administrative burdens while maintaining security. IAM solutions that prioritize user experience contribute to a more efficient and secure work environment.

IAM in the modern enterprise is a dynamic and evolving discipline that extends beyond traditional access control mechanisms. It encompasses identity verification, authentication, access governance, and privilege management to protect digital assets in an increasingly complex and distributed IT landscape. Organizations that invest in a robust IAM strategy can strengthen security, improve regulatory compliance, and enhance operational efficiency. As enterprises continue to adopt cloud-based services, mobile workforces, and automated systems, IAM will remain a foundational element of cybersecurity, ensuring that only the right users have access to the right resources at the right time.

Authentication and Authorization Fundamentals

Authentication and authorization are two foundational pillars of Identity and Access Management (IAM) that ensure secure access to digital resources. While they are often mentioned together, they serve distinct purposes. Authentication is the process of verifying a user's identity, ensuring that the individual attempting to access a system is who they claim to be. Authorization, on the other hand, determines what actions and resources an authenticated user is allowed to access. Together, these processes form the basis of access control in modern IT environments, protecting sensitive data and preventing unauthorized access.

Authentication begins with the validation of credentials that prove a user's identity. Traditional authentication methods rely on username and password combinations, which have long been the standard for accessing systems. However, passwords alone present significant security risks, as they can be easily compromised through phishing attacks, credential stuffing, and brute-force techniques. To address these vulnerabilities, organizations have adopted Multi-Factor Authentication (MFA), requiring users to provide additional verification factors before access is granted. MFA typically involves a combination of something the user knows, such as a password or PIN, something the user has, like a security token or smartphone app, and something the user is, such as biometric identifiers like fingerprints or facial recognition. By implementing MFA, enterprises significantly reduce the risk of unauthorized access, even if passwords are stolen or leaked.

Passwordless authentication is gaining traction as a more secure and user-friendly alternative to traditional authentication methods. Instead of relying on passwords, this approach leverages biometrics, cryptographic keys, or push notifications to verify user identity. Passwordless authentication eliminates common risks associated with weak or reused passwords while improving user experience. Organizations implementing passwordless authentication often use technologies such as Fast Identity Online (FIDO2) and WebAuthn, which enable secure authentication using hardware security keys, fingerprint scanners, or facial recognition. This method not only enhances security but also reduces the administrative burden of password resets and account recovery.

Single Sign-On (SSO) simplifies authentication by allowing users to access multiple applications with a single set of credentials. Instead of requiring users to log in separately to each system, SSO provides seamless access across connected services while maintaining security controls. Organizations integrate SSO with identity providers such as Microsoft Azure AD, Okta, or Google Identity to streamline authentication while enforcing security policies. By reducing password fatigue and minimizing the number of login credentials users need to manage, SSO enhances both security and productivity. However, SSO must be combined with strong authentication mechanisms, such as MFA, to prevent attackers from gaining access to multiple systems through a single compromised credential.

Authorization determines what actions a user can perform after authentication has been successfully completed. It ensures that users only have access to the resources necessary for their job functions, enforcing security principles such as least privilege and separation of duties. Authorization is typically implemented using access control models that define permissions based on roles, attributes, or policies.

Role-Based Access Control (RBAC) is one of the most widely used authorization models. RBAC assigns permissions based on predefined roles within an organization, ensuring that users only have access to resources relevant to their responsibilities. For example, a finance department employee might have access to accounting software but not to engineering databases. RBAC simplifies access management by grouping users into roles instead of assigning permissions individually, making it easier to enforce consistent security policies. However, organizations must regularly review role assignments to prevent privilege creep, where users accumulate excessive permissions over time due to job changes or temporary assignments.

Attribute-Based Access Control (ABAC) extends RBAC by incorporating additional attributes into access decisions. Instead of granting access solely based on predefined roles, ABAC considers dynamic attributes such as user location, device security posture, time of access, and sensitivity of the requested data. For example, a remote employee accessing a corporate application from an untrusted device might be required to provide additional authentication or might be restricted from downloading sensitive files. ABAC enables more granular and context-aware access control, allowing organizations to enforce security policies that adapt to real-time risk factors.

Just-In-Time (JIT) access is an advanced authorization technique that grants permissions only for the duration required to complete a specific task. Unlike traditional access control models that provide long-term or permanent access, JIT access minimizes security risks by ensuring that elevated privileges expire automatically after use. This approach is particularly valuable for privileged access management, where administrators, contractors, or support personnel require temporary access to sensitive systems. By implementing JIT access, organizations can reduce the risk of privilege misuse while maintaining operational efficiency.

Privileged Access Management (PAM) is an essential component of authorization that focuses on securing accounts with elevated privileges. Administrative accounts, root accounts, and service accounts have higher access rights than regular users, making them prime targets for cyberattacks. PAM solutions enforce strict access controls, requiring users to request privileged access through an approval workflow before granting temporary permissions. Additionally, PAM tools monitor and record privileged sessions, providing an audit trail for security and compliance purposes. By restricting and closely monitoring privileged access, organizations can mitigate the risks associated with insider threats and compromised credentials.

Access control policies define how authentication and authorization rules are enforced across an enterprise. Policies are typically governed by security frameworks such as the National Institute of Standards and Technology (NIST) Zero Trust Architecture, which emphasizes continuous verification and least privilege access. Organizations implement policy-based access control (PBAC) to enforce access rules dynamically, adjusting permissions based on real-time security assessments. For example, if a user logs in from a high-risk location or an untrusted device, access may be restricted or require additional verification steps. Policy-driven access control enhances security by continuously adapting to changing risk conditions.

Identity governance is closely tied to authentication and authorization, ensuring that access rights are granted, reviewed, and revoked in a secure and compliant manner. Organizations must conduct regular access reviews to validate that users have appropriate permissions and to remove unnecessary access. Automated identity governance solutions streamline this process, providing visibility into access patterns and detecting anomalies. Compliance regulations such as GDPR, HIPAA, and SOC 2 require organizations to implement strict identity controls, making authentication and authorization an integral part of regulatory compliance efforts.

Authentication and authorization are fundamental to securing enterprise systems, preventing unauthorized access, and enforcing access control policies. As cyber threats continue to evolve, organizations must implement strong authentication mechanisms, dynamic authorization models, and policy-driven access controls to protect their digital assets. By integrating advanced authentication technologies, enforcing least privilege access, and continuously monitoring access behavior, enterprises can build a resilient security framework that balances usability and security.

The Role of Multi-Factor Authentication (MFA)

Multi-Factor Authentication (MFA) is a critical security measure that enhances identity verification by requiring users to provide multiple forms of authentication before gaining access to systems, applications, or data. Traditional authentication methods relying solely on usernames and passwords have proven to be inadequate against modern cyber threats, as attackers can easily compromise credentials through phishing, brute-force attacks, and data breaches. MFA mitigates these risks by adding additional layers of security, ensuring that even if one authentication factor is compromised, unauthorized access remains difficult.

MFA operates by requiring users to provide two or more authentication factors from different categories: something they know, something they have, and something they are. The first factor, something they know, typically includes passwords, PINs, or security questions. The second factor, something they have, includes physical security tokens, mobile authentication apps, or smart cards. The third factor, something they are, includes biometrics such as fingerprints, facial recognition, or retina scans. By requiring authentication from at least two different categories, MFA significantly reduces the risk of unauthorized access and strengthens overall security posture.

The adoption of MFA has increased as organizations recognize its effectiveness in preventing account takeovers and unauthorized access. Cybercriminals frequently exploit weak passwords or stolen credentials to gain access to sensitive systems, but MFA provides an additional layer of protection that disrupts these attacks. Even if an attacker acquires a user's password, they would still need to bypass the second authentication factor, which is often tied to a physical device or biometric verification. This makes MFA an essential security control for enterprises, government agencies, financial institutions, and other organizations handling sensitive information.

MFA implementations vary depending on the security requirements and risk tolerance of an organization. The most common form of MFA is two-factor authentication (2FA), where users provide a password along with a secondary authentication factor, such as a one-time passcode (OTP) sent via SMS, email, or an authentication app. OTP-based authentication is widely used due to its simplicity and ease of deployment. However, SMS and email-based OTPs are susceptible to interception, SIM swapping, and phishing attacks, prompting organizations to adopt more secure alternatives such as mobile authentication apps and hardware security keys.

Authentication applications such as Google Authenticator, Microsoft Authenticator, and Authy generate time-based one-time passwords (TOTP) that expire after a short duration. These applications provide enhanced security compared to SMS-based OTPs, as they do not rely on telecommunications networks that can be compromised. Hardware security keys, such as YubiKeys or FIDO2-based authenticators, offer even stronger protection by requiring physical possession of the device to complete authentication. These keys use cryptographic authentication protocols that are resistant to phishing attacks, making them an ideal choice for high-security environments.

Biometric authentication is another powerful form of MFA that leverages unique biological characteristics to verify user identity. Fingerprint scanners, facial recognition, voice recognition, and iris scans are commonly used in biometric authentication systems. Biometrics offer a convenient and secure authentication method, as they eliminate the need for users to remember passwords or carry physical tokens. However, biometric authentication must be implemented with caution, as compromised biometric data cannot be changed like a password. Organizations employing biometrics must ensure that biometric data is encrypted and stored securely to prevent unauthorized access or misuse.

Adaptive MFA enhances traditional MFA by incorporating contextual risk analysis into authentication decisions. Instead of applying the same level of authentication across all login attempts, adaptive MFA dynamically adjusts authentication requirements based on factors such as user behavior, device reputation, geographic location, and network conditions. For example, if a user logs in from a recognized device in a trusted location, they may only be required to provide a password. However, if the same user attempts to log in from an unfamiliar device in a high-risk region, they may be prompted for additional authentication, such as a biometric scan or security key verification. This approach improves security while minimizing authentication friction for legitimate users.

MFA is a key component of Zero Trust security models, which assume that no user or device should be inherently trusted. In a Zero Trust environment, access to corporate resources is granted based on continuous authentication and risk assessment, rather than static credentials. MFA ensures that users are verified at multiple points, reducing the likelihood of unauthorized access. Organizations implementing Zero Trust policies often combine MFA with least privilege access controls and continuous monitoring to create a resilient security framework that adapts to evolving threats.

The implementation of MFA in enterprise environments requires careful planning to balance security with usability. While MFA strengthens security, excessive authentication requirements can frustrate users and lead to productivity challenges. Organizations must adopt an MFA strategy that aligns with user workflows, providing seamless authentication experiences without compromising security. Single Sign-On (SSO) solutions integrated with MFA allow users to authenticate once and access multiple applications securely, reducing authentication fatigue. Passwordless authentication methods, such as biometric authentication and FIDO2 security keys, further improve user experience by eliminating password-related barriers.

Regulatory compliance and industry standards increasingly mandate the use of MFA to protect sensitive information. Regulations such as the General Data Protection Regulation (GDPR), the Health Insurance Portability and Accountability Act (HIPAA), and the Payment Card Industry Data Security Standard (PCI DSS) require organizations to implement strong authentication mechanisms to protect user identities and prevent unauthorized data access. Financial institutions and critical infrastructure providers are also required to enforce MFA for privileged accounts and remote access. By adopting MFA, organizations not only enhance security but also ensure compliance with legal and regulatory requirements.

Despite its effectiveness, MFA is not a standalone solution and must be combined with other security measures to provide comprehensive protection. Attackers continuously develop new techniques to bypass MFA, including social engineering, MFA fatigue attacks, and session hijacking. Organizations must educate users on the importance of verifying authentication requests and recognizing phishing attempts that attempt to steal MFA credentials. Security teams should also implement session monitoring and anomaly detection to identify suspicious authentication attempts and take appropriate action.

MFA plays a crucial role in securing modern digital environments, protecting user identities, and preventing unauthorized access. As cyber threats evolve, organizations must continue to refine their MFA strategies, adopting more advanced authentication methods that balance security with usability. By integrating MFA with Zero Trust security frameworks, adaptive authentication, and continuous monitoring, enterprises can create a resilient security posture that defends against both internal and external threats.

Identity Governance and Administration (IGA)

Identity Governance and Administration (IGA) is a critical component of Identity and Access Management (IAM) that focuses on managing user identities, enforcing access policies, and ensuring compliance with regulatory requirements. As enterprises grow and their digital environments become more complex, maintaining control over user identities and their associated privileges is essential for reducing security risks and preventing unauthorized access. IGA provides organizations with the tools and processes necessary to automate identity lifecycle management, enforce least privilege access, and conduct access reviews to maintain security and regulatory compliance.

The foundation of IGA lies in identity lifecycle management, which governs how user identities are created, modified, and deactivated throughout their time in an organization. When a new employee, contractor, or partner joins an enterprise, their digital identity must be provisioned with the appropriate access rights to perform their job functions. Automated provisioning ensures that new users receive access to necessary applications and resources without unnecessary delays. Similarly, when an employee changes roles, their access permissions must be updated accordingly to reflect their new responsibilities. Automated role changes help prevent privilege accumulation, where users retain access to resources that are no longer relevant to their role. When an employee leaves the organization, deprovisioning processes ensure that their access is revoked promptly to reduce the risk of orphaned accounts that could be exploited by malicious actors.

Role-Based Access Control (RBAC) is a fundamental aspect of IGA that simplifies identity management by assigning permissions based on predefined roles. Instead of granting access on an individual basis, RBAC groups users into roles with specific permissions, ensuring that employees only have access to the resources necessary for their job functions. This structured approach reduces administrative overhead and improves security by minimizing excessive privileges. However, role management must be regularly reviewed to prevent role sprawl, where an excessive number of roles are created, leading to complexity and security gaps. Organizations implementing IGA use role mining techniques to analyze existing permissions and define optimal role structures that align with business needs.

Attribute-Based Access Control (ABAC) extends the capabilities of RBAC by incorporating dynamic attributes into access decisions. Instead of relying solely on static roles, ABAC evaluates contextual attributes such as user location, device security posture, time of access, and job function to determine authorization. This approach enables more granular and adaptive access control policies that enhance security while maintaining operational flexibility. IGA solutions integrate ABAC with identity governance frameworks to enforce policy-driven access management, ensuring that access rights are granted based on real-time risk assessments.

Access certification is a critical function of IGA that ensures users maintain only the necessary permissions required for their roles. Organizations conduct periodic access reviews, requiring managers and system owners to verify whether users still need access to specific resources. These reviews help identify excessive or outdated privileges that could pose security risks. Automating the access certification process reduces administrative burden and improves accuracy by providing real-time insights into user access patterns. IGA solutions facilitate these reviews by generating reports, tracking approvals, and enforcing corrective actions when unnecessary access is detected.

Compliance and regulatory mandates drive the need for strong identity governance practices. Organizations must adhere to industry regulations such as the General Data Protection Regulation (GDPR), the Health Insurance Portability and Accountability Act (HIPAA), the Sarbanes-Oxley Act (SOX), and the Payment Card Industry Data Security Standard (PCI DSS), which require strict access controls and identity management policies. IGA solutions help organizations achieve compliance by providing audit trails, enforcing security policies, and generating compliance reports. By implementing automated identity governance processes, enterprises can demonstrate compliance with regulatory requirements while reducing the risk of security violations and financial penalties.

Privileged Access Management (PAM) is closely related to IGA, as it focuses on securing accounts with elevated privileges. Administrative accounts, system accounts, and privileged users require additional security controls to prevent misuse and insider threats. IGA solutions integrate with PAM tools to enforce policies that restrict and monitor privileged access, ensuring that elevated permissions are granted only when necessary and revoked when no longer needed. Just-In-Time (JIT) access provisioning further enhances security by providing temporary access to privileged accounts based on approval workflows, reducing the risk of persistent administrative privileges being exploited.

Identity analytics and risk-based access control play a significant role in modern IGA implementations. Traditional identity governance processes relied on static rules and periodic reviews, but evolving security threats require continuous monitoring and adaptive risk assessment. Identity analytics leverage machine learning and artificial intelligence to detect anomalies in user behavior, identifying potential security risks such as privilege escalation, unusual login attempts, and unauthorized access attempts. Risk-based access control dynamically adjusts access permissions based on contextual risk factors, such as failed login attempts, geolocation anomalies, and device security status. By integrating identity analytics with IGA, organizations can proactively detect and mitigate security threats before they result in data breaches.

IGA also plays a crucial role in managing third-party and external identities. Organizations frequently grant access to contractors, suppliers, and business partners who require access to enterprise systems. However, managing third-party identities presents security challenges, as external users may not be subject to the same internal security policies as employees. IGA solutions enforce strict access controls for third-party identities, ensuring that external users are granted only temporary and limited access based on predefined policies. Regular access reviews and automated deprovisioning prevent unauthorized access after a third-party engagement ends.

Self-service identity management capabilities enhance user experience while maintaining security controls. IGA solutions enable users to request access to applications and resources through self-service portals, reducing the burden on IT and security teams. Automated approval workflows ensure that access requests are reviewed and granted based on predefined policies, streamlining access management without compromising security. Additionally, self-service password reset capabilities allow users to reset their passwords securely without IT intervention, reducing helpdesk costs and minimizing downtime caused by forgotten credentials.

The integration of IGA with cloud environments is essential for modern enterprises managing hybrid IT infrastructures. Cloud adoption has introduced new challenges in identity governance, as users access applications and data across multiple cloud platforms. IGA solutions extend governance policies to cloud-based identities, enforcing consistent access controls across on-premises and cloud environments. Cloud identity governance platforms provide centralized visibility into user access, automating identity lifecycle management and ensuring compliance with security policies. As organizations continue to migrate to cloud-based applications and services, integrating IGA with cloud IAM solutions becomes a critical aspect of enterprise security strategy.

IGA is a vital component of enterprise security and compliance, providing organizations with the tools needed to manage identities, enforce access policies, and mitigate security risks. By automating identity lifecycle management, conducting access reviews, enforcing least privilege access, and leveraging identity analytics, organizations can enhance security while maintaining regulatory compliance. As the threat landscape evolves, IGA solutions will continue to play a key role in ensuring that users have the appropriate access they need while protecting sensitive data from unauthorized access and cyber threats.

Privileged Access Management (PAM)

Privileged Access Management (PAM) is a critical security discipline within Identity and Access Management (IAM) that focuses on controlling, monitoring, and securing elevated access to critical systems and sensitive data. Privileged accounts, such as system administrators, database administrators, and network engineers, have significantly higher levels of access than regular users. If these accounts are compromised, attackers can move laterally through an organization's infrastructure, escalate privileges, and gain control over sensitive systems. PAM solutions help organizations enforce security policies that minimize the risk associated with privileged accounts while ensuring that administrative tasks can be performed securely and efficiently.

Privileged accounts exist across all enterprise environments, including on-premises data centers, cloud platforms, and hybrid infrastructures. These accounts include human users with administrative roles as well as machine identities such as service accounts, scripts, and automated processes. Traditional access management solutions focus primarily on standard user accounts, but PAM is designed to address the unique risks associated with privileged access. A lack of proper controls over privileged accounts can lead to security breaches, compliance violations, and operational disruptions. Attackers frequently target privileged credentials through phishing, credential stuffing, and malware-based attacks to gain unauthorized access to an organization's most critical assets.

The core principle of PAM is the enforcement of least privilege access, ensuring that privileged users have only the permissions necessary to perform their tasks. Instead of granting permanent administrative rights, PAM solutions implement Just-In-Time (JIT) access, which provides time-limited access to privileged accounts based on need. This reduces the attack surface by eliminating persistent administrative privileges that could be exploited by attackers. When a user requires privileged access, they must submit a request, which is subject to approval and audit before access is granted. Once the task is completed, the elevated access is revoked automatically, preventing privilege accumulation and reducing the risk of misuse.

Credential vaulting is a key component of PAM, designed to secure and manage privileged credentials. Instead of allowing privileged users to maintain static credentials, PAM solutions store administrative passwords in a secure vault, encrypting them and enforcing strict access controls. Users retrieve passwords from the vault when needed, and the system automatically rotates credentials after each use to prevent unauthorized reuse. This ensures that even if a password is compromised, it cannot be used to gain persistent access. Automated credential rotation eliminates the risks associated with password sharing and hardcoded credentials, reducing the likelihood of unauthorized access.

Session monitoring and recording provide real-time visibility into privileged user activities. PAM solutions track and log every action taken by privileged users, creating an audit trail that can be reviewed for compliance and security purposes. Some PAM systems also support live session monitoring, allowing security teams to observe privileged sessions in real time and intervene if suspicious activity is detected. Recording privileged sessions ensures accountability, discourages misuse, and provides forensic evidence in the event of a security incident. These audit logs are essential for meeting regulatory compliance requirements, as many industry standards mandate strict oversight of privileged access.

Privileged access policies enforce rules and restrictions on how privileged accounts can be used. Organizations define access control policies that specify which users can access specific systems, what actions they can perform, and under what conditions access is granted. Context-aware access controls enhance security by evaluating factors such as user location, device security posture, and login behavior before granting privileged access. For example, if a system administrator attempts to log in from an unfamiliar location, the PAM system may require additional authentication or block access entirely. By integrating risk-based access controls, PAM solutions reduce the likelihood of unauthorized access while maintaining operational flexibility.

Cloud environments introduce new challenges in privileged access management, as organizations adopt multi-cloud and hybrid architectures that require secure access to cloud-based administrative consoles, APIs, and virtual machines. PAM solutions extend governance to cloud environments, ensuring that cloud administrators and service accounts adhere to the same security policies as on-premises privileged users. Cloud-native PAM solutions integrate with identity providers, enforcing strong authentication and access controls for privileged users managing cloud infrastructure. This is especially important in cloud environments where misconfigurations and excessive permissions can expose sensitive data to external threats.

Third-party access poses another significant risk in privileged access management. Organizations frequently grant external vendors, contractors, and partners temporary access to internal systems for maintenance, support, and collaboration. However, unmanaged third-party access can introduce security vulnerabilities, as external users may not follow the same security policies as internal employees. PAM solutions enforce strict access controls for third-party users, requiring them to authenticate through secure access portals, use MFA, and follow Just-In-Time access principles. Session recording and monitoring ensure that all third-party activities are logged and reviewed to prevent unauthorized changes or data breaches.

Insider threats remain a major concern for privileged access security. Employees with administrative access may misuse their privileges for personal gain, sabotage, or espionage. PAM solutions mitigate insider threats by enforcing the principle of least privilege, implementing role-based access controls, and monitoring privileged user activities for suspicious behavior. Behavioral analytics and anomaly detection help identify deviations from normal user activity, triggering alerts when unauthorized actions are attempted. By continuously monitoring privileged users and enforcing security policies, organizations can detect and prevent malicious insider activity before it leads to significant damage.

Automation and artificial intelligence enhance PAM capabilities by enabling proactive security measures. AI-powered PAM solutions analyze privileged access patterns, detect anomalies, and predict potential security threats before they escalate. Machine learning models help organizations identify excessive privileges, detect inactive privileged accounts, and enforce policy-driven access controls. Automated remediation workflows streamline incident response by revoking suspicious access, rotating credentials, and isolating compromised accounts in real time. By integrating AI and automation, PAM solutions reduce administrative overhead while strengthening security defenses against advanced threats.

Regulatory compliance mandates the implementation of strong privileged access controls to protect sensitive data and prevent unauthorized access. Industry regulations such as GDPR, HIPAA, PCI DSS, and SOX require organizations to enforce strict security measures for privileged accounts, including MFA, session monitoring, and access audits. PAM solutions provide organizations with the tools needed to achieve compliance by ensuring that privileged access is managed, documented, and secured according to industry best practices. Failure to implement PAM controls can result in financial penalties, reputational damage, and increased vulnerability to cyberattacks.

Privileged Access Management is an essential component of cybersecurity, protecting organizations from external threats, insider risks, and compliance violations. By enforcing least privilege access, securing privileged credentials, monitoring administrative sessions, and integrating with cloud environments, PAM solutions reduce the risk of privilege abuse and unauthorized access. As cyber threats continue to evolve, organizations must prioritize the implementation of PAM to safeguard critical assets, enforce security policies, and maintain a resilient security posture.

Role-Based Access Control (RBAC) and Zero Trust

Role-Based Access Control (RBAC) is a widely used access management framework that assigns permissions to users based on predefined roles within an organization. Instead of granting individual access to specific systems or resources on a case-by-case basis, RBAC groups users with similar job functions into roles that define their level of access. This structured approach simplifies access management, enhances security, and ensures that users only have the permissions necessary to perform their duties. As organizations adopt Zero Trust security models, RBAC plays a critical role in enforcing least privilege access, reducing excessive permissions, and ensuring that trust is continuously verified before granting access.

RBAC operates by defining roles based on business functions and associating access privileges with each role. For example, an organization may create roles such as "HR Manager," "Finance Analyst," "IT Administrator," and "Customer Support Representative," each with specific access rights to applications, databases, and services. When a new employee joins the organization, they are assigned a role that automatically grants them the necessary permissions. This eliminates the need for administrators to manually configure access for each user, reducing administrative overhead and the risk of human error.

One of the primary benefits of RBAC is its ability to enforce the principle of least privilege, ensuring that users do not have more access than they need. Without RBAC, organizations often struggle with permission sprawl, where users accumulate excessive privileges over time due to role changes, temporary assignments, or misconfigured access policies. This creates security vulnerabilities that attackers can exploit to gain unauthorized access to critical systems. RBAC mitigates this risk by structuring access in a way that aligns with business needs while preventing privilege escalation. Regular role reviews help organizations maintain security by identifying and removing unnecessary permissions.

Zero Trust security models emphasize continuous verification, strict access controls, and the elimination of implicit trust within networks and systems. Unlike traditional perimeter-based security approaches that assume internal users and devices are trustworthy, Zero Trust operates on the principle that every access request must be verified, regardless of the user's location or device. RBAC aligns with Zero Trust by ensuring that access is granted based on well-defined policies rather than assumed trust. Users are assigned roles based on their identity attributes, job functions, and business requirements, and their access is continuously evaluated to prevent unauthorized actions.

Dynamic role assignment is an important aspect of integrating RBAC with Zero Trust. Traditional RBAC models rely on static role assignments, where users are manually assigned roles when they join an organization. However, Zero Trust requires a more adaptive approach, where roles are dynamically adjusted based on real-time risk assessments and contextual factors. For example, if a user logs in from an untrusted location or an unmanaged device, their assigned role may be temporarily restricted to limit access to sensitive systems. Adaptive RBAC ensures that users maintain appropriate levels of access based on evolving security conditions.

Attribute-Based Access Control (ABAC) enhances RBAC by incorporating contextual attributes into access decisions. While RBAC assigns permissions based on predefined roles, ABAC considers factors such as user location, device security posture, time of access, and authentication method before granting or denying access. Integrating ABAC with RBAC strengthens Zero Trust implementations by making access control policies more granular and responsive to real-time security risks. Organizations can define policies that enforce additional authentication requirements or restrict access based on situational risk factors, ensuring that access permissions remain aligned with security policies.

RBAC is also crucial for enforcing least privilege access in multi-cloud and hybrid IT environments. As organizations adopt cloud services, software-as-a-service (SaaS) applications, and remote work models, managing access across diverse platforms becomes challenging. Cloud identity providers, such as Microsoft Azure AD, AWS IAM, and Google Cloud IAM, support RBAC-based policies to restrict access to cloud resources. By implementing RBAC in cloud environments, organizations ensure that users only have the permissions necessary to perform their tasks while minimizing the risk of cloud misconfigurations that could lead to data breaches.

Privileged Access Management (PAM) integrates with RBAC to provide additional security for accounts with elevated privileges. Administrative and system-level accounts require strict access controls to prevent unauthorized modifications to critical infrastructure. PAM solutions enforce Just-In-Time (JIT) access for privileged roles, ensuring that elevated permissions are granted only when needed and revoked after use. By combining RBAC with PAM, organizations prevent persistent administrative access, reducing the risk of insider threats and compromised credentials.

RBAC also plays a role in compliance and regulatory requirements. Many industry standards, such as GDPR, HIPAA, and SOX, mandate strict access controls to protect sensitive data and prevent unauthorized access. RBAC simplifies compliance by providing clear role definitions, access policies, and audit logs that demonstrate adherence to security best practices. Automated access reviews help organizations verify that users have the correct permissions, identify privilege violations, and ensure compliance with security policies.

Zero Trust architecture requires continuous monitoring and auditing of access activities to detect anomalies and prevent security incidents. RBAC, when integrated with identity analytics and machine learning, enables organizations to analyze user behavior patterns and detect deviations that may indicate compromised accounts or malicious activity. For example, if a user assigned to a "Finance Analyst" role suddenly attempts to access engineering databases, security systems can flag this behavior as suspicious and trigger an investigation. By combining RBAC with real-time analytics, organizations strengthen their Zero Trust security posture and reduce the risk of unauthorized access.

Implementing RBAC effectively requires a structured approach to role design, policy enforcement, and continuous access management. Organizations must conduct role discovery exercises to identify business functions, define appropriate roles, and map permissions accordingly. Overcomplicating role structures with excessive granularity can lead to management challenges, while overly broad roles may introduce security risks. A balanced RBAC implementation ensures that access is both secure and manageable.

RBAC is a fundamental access control model that aligns with Zero Trust principles by enforcing least privilege access, dynamic role assignments, and continuous verification of access permissions. By integrating RBAC with adaptive authentication, identity analytics, and cloud security policies, organizations create a robust security framework that minimizes access risks and prevents unauthorized privilege escalation. As Zero Trust adoption continues to grow, RBAC remains an essential tool for organizations seeking to implement secure and efficient access control strategies.

Attribute-Based Access Control (ABAC) in IAM

Attribute-Based Access Control (ABAC) is an advanced access control model that enhances security and flexibility in Identity and Access Management (IAM) by making access decisions based on attributes rather than static roles or predefined permissions. Unlike Role-Based Access Control (RBAC), which assigns permissions based on fixed roles, ABAC dynamically evaluates contextual factors such as user attributes, resource characteristics, environmental conditions, and security posture before granting or denying access. This dynamic approach enables organizations to enforce more granular and adaptive access control policies, aligning with the principles of Zero Trust and least privilege access.

ABAC operates by defining access control policies that evaluate multiple attributes in real-time. These attributes can be categorized into four primary types: subject attributes, which describe the user requesting access; object attributes, which define the resource being accessed; action attributes, which specify what operation the user wants to perform; and environmental attributes, which include contextual factors such as time of access, geographic location, and device security posture. By evaluating these attributes together, ABAC enables organizations to enforce sophisticated access control rules that adjust dynamically based on risk levels and operational needs.

One of the primary advantages of ABAC is its ability to enforce fine-grained access control. Traditional access models such as RBAC rely on predefined roles, which can lead to permission sprawl and excessive privileges if roles are not carefully managed. ABAC eliminates the need for excessive role definitions by allowing access policies to be based on a combination of attributes rather than rigid role assignments. For example, an organization using RBAC might have to create separate roles for "Finance Manager," "Finance Analyst," and "Finance Contractor" to differentiate access levels. With ABAC, a single policy can evaluate attributes such as job title, employment status, and department, dynamically adjusting permissions based on real-time conditions without requiring separate roles for each variation.

ABAC enhances security by incorporating real-time risk assessment into access control decisions. Since ABAC policies consider environmental attributes such as device security posture, IP address, and geolocation, access requests can be evaluated in context. If an employee attempts to access sensitive financial data from a company-issued laptop within the corporate network, access might be granted without additional verification. However, if the same employee attempts to access the same data from an untrusted device in a foreign country, ABAC policies can enforce additional authentication measures, restrict certain actions, or deny access altogether. This contextual decision-making aligns with Zero Trust principles, ensuring that access is granted based on real-time security conditions rather than static permissions.

Organizations implementing ABAC benefit from increased operational flexibility, as access policies can be adapted to accommodate evolving business requirements. In dynamic work environments where users frequently change roles, take on temporary assignments, or collaborate across departments, ABAC ensures that access permissions are automatically adjusted based on real-time user attributes. This eliminates the need for IT administrators to manually update access rights whenever employees change positions or take on additional responsibilities. By automating access decisions through ABAC, organizations reduce administrative overhead while maintaining a high level of security and compliance.

ABAC plays a crucial role in securing cloud environments, where users, devices, and applications access resources from multiple locations and platforms. Cloud identity providers such as AWS IAM, Azure Active Directory, and Google Cloud IAM support attribute-based access policies to regulate access across cloud applications and services. Organizations using ABAC in cloud environments can define access control rules that evaluate user identity attributes, device trust levels, and session risk scores before granting access. This ensures that cloud resources are protected from unauthorized access while allowing legitimate users to work efficiently from any location.

Compliance and regulatory requirements drive the need for stronger access control mechanisms, making ABAC an essential tool for organizations subject to data protection laws such as GDPR, HIPAA, and PCI DSS. ABAC helps organizations enforce compliance policies by restricting access to sensitive data based on user attributes such as job function, clearance level, and regulatory status. For example, a healthcare organization can implement ABAC policies that allow doctors to view patient medical records but restrict nurses from modifying them unless specific conditions are met. Similarly, a financial institution can use ABAC to enforce segregation of duties, ensuring that employees in certain roles do not have conflicting access privileges that could enable fraud or data breaches.

The integration of ABAC with IAM solutions enables organizations to implement policy-driven access control frameworks that align with business objectives and security requirements. Modern IAM platforms support ABAC by providing policy engines that evaluate attributes in real time, enforcing access rules dynamically without requiring manual intervention. These IAM solutions integrate with identity governance tools, security analytics platforms, and compliance monitoring systems to ensure that access policies remain effective and up to date. By leveraging ABAC within IAM, organizations can create adaptive security policies that enhance protection while maintaining operational efficiency.

ABAC also enhances data security by applying attribute-based controls to file access, database queries, and API interactions. Organizations handling sensitive data can define policies that regulate access based on data sensitivity levels and user attributes. For example, an ABAC policy can restrict access to confidential financial reports to employees with a "Finance Director" attribute while allowing read-only access to employees with a "Finance Analyst" attribute. In API security, ABAC ensures that service accounts and applications only access specific endpoints based on attributes such as API key ownership, request type, and encryption status. This prevents unauthorized data access and reduces the risk of API exploitation by malicious actors.

Despite its advantages, implementing ABAC requires careful planning and a well-structured approach to attribute management. Organizations must define a clear taxonomy of attributes, establish data governance policies, and integrate attribute sources such as human resources systems, directory services, and security monitoring tools. ABAC policies should be designed with scalability in mind, ensuring that access control rules remain manageable as organizations grow and adapt to new security challenges. By combining ABAC with automation and AI-driven analytics, organizations can continuously refine access policies, detect anomalous access patterns, and improve overall security posture.

ABAC is a powerful access control model that enhances IAM by providing dynamic, context-aware security policies that adapt to real-time risk conditions. By evaluating multiple attributes before granting access, ABAC enforces least privilege principles, strengthens Zero Trust security, and improves regulatory compliance. As enterprises continue to adopt cloud services, hybrid IT environments, and remote work models, ABAC offers a scalable and flexible solution to manage access rights effectively while minimizing security risks.

Just-In-Time (JIT) Access Management

Just-In-Time (JIT) Access Management is a security model that grants users and applications access to critical resources only when needed and for a limited duration. Unlike traditional access management models, where users and administrators often have persistent access to sensitive systems, JIT access ensures that elevated permissions are provisioned temporarily and revoked once the task is completed. This approach significantly reduces the attack surface by minimizing the exposure of privileged credentials, preventing unauthorized access, and limiting the risk of insider threats and privilege escalation attacks.

In traditional IT environments, users with administrative or elevated privileges often retain their access indefinitely, even when they do not actively require it. This leads to the accumulation of excessive permissions, known as privilege creep, which increases security risks. If an attacker compromises an account with standing privileges, they can use it to move laterally within the network, escalate privileges, and access sensitive data. JIT access mitigates these risks by eliminating standing privileges and enforcing temporary access only when required. Instead of permanently assigning users to privileged roles, organizations implement approval workflows that grant access dynamically based on business needs.

JIT access operates through multiple provisioning methods, including on-demand access requests, automated access elevation, and ephemeral credentials. On-demand access requests require users to submit a justification for elevated access, which is then reviewed and approved before granting permissions. This ensures that access is granted only when a legitimate business case exists. Automated access elevation occurs when a system detects a valid need for elevated privileges based on predefined rules and conditions, such as specific job functions or scheduled maintenance tasks. Ephemeral credentials provide temporary access tokens or passwords that automatically expire after use, preventing credentials from being reused or exploited.

Privileged Access Management (PAM) solutions integrate JIT access to enhance security for administrative accounts, system credentials, and critical infrastructure. Traditional PAM models store and rotate privileged credentials within secure vaults, ensuring that only authorized users can retrieve them. When combined with JIT access, PAM systems enforce time-limited access policies, ensuring that privileged accounts cannot be accessed outside of approved sessions. Users requesting privileged access must authenticate through multiple factors and obtain explicit approval before receiving a temporary credential. Once the session ends, the credential expires, and access is revoked automatically. This reduces the risk of persistent administrative access being exploited by attackers or malicious insiders.

JIT access is particularly valuable in cloud environments, where organizations manage access to cloud workloads, virtual machines, and SaaS applications across multiple platforms. Cloud Identity and Access Management (IAM) services support JIT access policies that dynamically grant permissions based on workload demands. Instead of assigning long-term access to cloud resources, organizations implement temporary access policies that provision permissions for specific tasks, such as database maintenance, application deployment, or security audits. Cloud providers such as AWS, Microsoft Azure, and Google Cloud offer JIT access mechanisms that integrate with identity providers to enforce least privilege access while maintaining operational agility.

The integration of JIT access with Zero Trust security models enhances access control by ensuring that no user, device, or application is granted implicit trust. Zero Trust operates on the principle of continuous verification, requiring access requests to be evaluated based on real-time risk assessments. JIT access aligns with this model by ensuring that privileged access is granted only when necessary and verified at multiple checkpoints. Instead of assuming that internal users are inherently trustworthy, Zero Trust policies enforce strict authentication and authorization measures before granting temporary permissions. This prevents attackers from exploiting persistent privileges to escalate access and compromise sensitive systems.

Automation plays a crucial role in the successful implementation of JIT access, reducing administrative burden while maintaining security. Organizations use automated workflows to streamline access requests, approvals, and revocation processes. Identity governance solutions integrate with JIT access to enforce policy-based access controls, ensuring that users receive the correct permissions based on contextual factors such as job role, department, and security posture. By leveraging AI-driven analytics, organizations can detect abnormal access patterns and automatically trigger remediation actions, such as revoking access or requiring additional authentication.

JIT access also enhances security for DevOps and software development environments, where developers and IT teams require temporary access to infrastructure and code repositories. Instead of assigning persistent permissions to development and production environments, organizations implement JIT access controls that grant short-term privileges for tasks such as deploying code, modifying configurations, or troubleshooting issues. This prevents unauthorized code changes, reduces insider threats, and ensures that only approved users can make modifications to critical systems. By integrating JIT access with DevOps tools and CI/CD pipelines, organizations enforce security policies without disrupting development workflows.

Compliance and regulatory frameworks emphasize the importance of controlling privileged access, making JIT access an essential component of enterprise security strategies. Regulations such as GDPR, HIPAA, PCI DSS, and SOX require organizations to enforce strict access controls, monitor privileged sessions, and minimize unnecessary access to sensitive data. JIT access aligns with these requirements by ensuring that access is granted based on business necessity and automatically revoked after use. Organizations implementing JIT access can generate audit logs and compliance reports that demonstrate adherence to security policies, reducing the risk of regulatory violations and potential financial penalties.

User experience is a critical consideration in JIT access implementations, as overly restrictive access policies can hinder productivity and lead to user frustration. To balance security and usability, organizations design JIT access workflows that provide seamless access while maintaining strong authentication controls. Self-service portals allow users to request temporary access without requiring manual IT intervention, accelerating approval processes and reducing delays. Adaptive authentication mechanisms further enhance user experience by dynamically adjusting access requirements based on real-time risk assessments, minimizing friction while ensuring security.

JIT access strengthens identity and access management by enforcing temporary and controlled access to sensitive systems, reducing the risk of privilege abuse and unauthorized access. By integrating JIT access with privileged access management, cloud security policies, and Zero Trust architectures, organizations enhance their security posture while maintaining operational efficiency. As cyber threats continue to evolve, JIT access remains a critical security measure for protecting enterprise resources, enforcing least privilege access, and preventing unauthorized privilege escalation.

Adaptive Access Control in Zero Trust

Adaptive Access Control is a fundamental component of the Zero Trust security model, allowing organizations to dynamically adjust access decisions based on real-time risk assessments. Unlike traditional access control methods that rely on static permissions and predefined roles, Adaptive Access Control continuously evaluates user behavior, device security posture, network conditions, and contextual factors before granting or denying access. This approach aligns with Zero Trust principles, ensuring that no entity—whether internal or external—is inherently trusted. Instead, access is granted conditionally and reassessed throughout a user's session to prevent unauthorized access and minimize security risks.

Zero Trust operates on the assumption that threats can originate from both inside and outside the organization's perimeter. In traditional security models, access was granted based on predefined roles, assuming that users within the corporate network were trustworthy. However, with the rise of remote work, cloud computing, and sophisticated cyber threats, static access controls are no longer sufficient. Adaptive Access Control enables organizations to implement a dynamic security framework that continuously evaluates risk factors and enforces the principle of least privilege. By leveraging real-time data and machine learning, Adaptive Access Control adjusts access permissions based on evolving security conditions, reducing the likelihood of data breaches and unauthorized activity.

The core functionality of Adaptive Access Control relies on contextual risk analysis. Before granting access, the system evaluates various factors, including user identity, device security status, geographic location, login behavior, and network risk level. If a user attempts to access corporate resources from a trusted device within a recognized network, access may be granted with minimal friction. However, if the same user tries to log in from an unknown location using an untrusted device, the system may prompt for additional authentication, restrict access to sensitive data, or block the request entirely. This dynamic decision-making process ensures that access permissions are tailored to the risk level of each request.

Device security posture plays a crucial role in Adaptive Access Control, ensuring that only compliant and secure devices are allowed to access corporate systems. Organizations define security requirements for devices, such as updated antivirus software, encrypted storage, and compliance with corporate security policies. If a device fails to meet these requirements, access can be restricted or redirected to a remediation process before granting permission. This prevents compromised or unpatched devices from introducing security vulnerabilities into the network. Endpoint detection and response (EDR) solutions integrate with Adaptive Access Control to provide real-time visibility into device health and detect potential threats before access is granted.

User behavior analytics (UBA) enhances Adaptive Access Control by detecting anomalies in user activity and access patterns. Traditional authentication mechanisms verify a user's identity at the beginning of a session but do not continuously monitor activity after login. Adaptive Access Control extends security beyond initial authentication by analyzing behavioral patterns such as login frequency, access times, and application usage. If a user exhibits unusual behavior—such as accessing sensitive data outside normal working hours or attempting to download large amounts of information—the system can trigger additional verification steps or revoke access in real time. This proactive approach helps prevent insider threats, compromised account usage, and unauthorized data exfiltration.

Multi-Factor Authentication (MFA) is a critical component of Adaptive Access Control, ensuring that users verify their identity through multiple authentication factors before gaining access. However, static MFA policies that require authentication for every login attempt can create friction for users. Adaptive MFA dynamically adjusts authentication requirements based on risk levels. For example, if a user logs in from a familiar device and location, they may only need to enter a password. If the same user attempts to access sensitive data from a high-risk location, the system may require biometric authentication or a one-time passcode sent to a trusted device. This adaptive approach balances security with user experience, reducing authentication fatigue while maintaining strong protection against unauthorized access.

Geo-fencing and location-based access controls further enhance Adaptive Access Control by restricting access based on geographic boundaries. Organizations can define policies that allow access only from specific regions or trusted locations. If a user attempts to log in from a country where the organization does not operate, the system can automatically block the request or enforce stricter authentication measures. Geo-fencing is particularly useful for preventing credential abuse by attackers who obtain stolen usernames and passwords but attempt to access systems from unrecognized locations. By leveraging geographic data, organizations can add an additional layer of security to their Zero Trust framework.

Network and session risk assessment is another key aspect of Adaptive Access Control. Organizations analyze network traffic, connection types, and IP reputation to determine whether an access request originates from a secure or high-risk network. If a user logs in from a corporate VPN or a trusted home network, access may be granted with minimal restrictions. However, if the request originates from a public Wi-Fi network or a known malicious IP address, the system may require additional verification or deny access altogether. Continuous session monitoring ensures that even after authentication, user activity is analyzed for anomalies, and access permissions are adjusted dynamically based on emerging threats.

Adaptive Access Control integrates with Zero Trust Network Access (ZTNA) solutions, providing secure access to applications and services without relying on traditional VPNs. Unlike VPNs, which grant broad network access once authenticated, ZTNA enforces granular access controls based on identity and security posture. Adaptive Access Control policies ensure that users can access only the applications and data they need, reducing the risk of lateral movement within the network. This approach enhances security for remote workforces and cloud-based environments, ensuring that access decisions are based on continuous risk evaluation rather than static permissions.

Compliance and regulatory requirements drive the need for organizations to implement strong access controls, making Adaptive Access Control an essential tool for meeting security standards. Regulations such as GDPR, HIPAA, and PCI DSS mandate strict identity verification and access management policies to protect sensitive data. Adaptive Access Control helps organizations enforce compliance by ensuring that access decisions are based on real-time risk assessments, providing audit trails for security incidents, and dynamically restricting access to regulated information. By implementing continuous authentication and contextual access policies, organizations can meet compliance requirements while reducing exposure to security threats.

The implementation of Adaptive Access Control requires a combination of advanced security technologies, including identity analytics, behavioral monitoring, artificial intelligence, and automation. Organizations must define risk-based policies, integrate real-time threat intelligence, and continuously refine access rules based on evolving security trends. Automation reduces administrative overhead by dynamically adjusting access permissions without requiring manual intervention, allowing security teams to focus on more critical threats. By leveraging AI-driven security analytics, organizations can improve threat detection, enhance decision-making, and enforce Zero Trust principles effectively.

Adaptive Access Control is a cornerstone of modern cybersecurity, enabling organizations to enforce Zero Trust security by continuously evaluating risk factors, adjusting access permissions dynamically, and preventing unauthorized activity. By incorporating behavioral analytics, contextual authentication, and continuous monitoring, organizations strengthen their security posture while ensuring a seamless user experience. As cyber threats become more sophisticated, Adaptive Access Control remains a vital strategy for reducing security risks, enforcing least privilege access, and maintaining compliance in an increasingly complex digital landscape.

Continuous Monitoring and Risk-Based Authentication

Continuous Monitoring and Risk-Based Authentication are critical components of modern cybersecurity and Identity and Access Management (IAM) frameworks. As cyber threats become more sophisticated, static authentication methods and periodic security checks are no longer sufficient to protect sensitive data and resources. Continuous monitoring ensures that user behavior, system activities, and access patterns are constantly evaluated for anomalies, while risk-based authentication dynamically adjusts authentication requirements based on real-time risk assessments. Together, these strategies enable organizations to proactively detect threats, enforce least privilege access, and minimize the likelihood of unauthorized access.

Traditional authentication models rely on one-time identity verification during login. Once authenticated, users often maintain their access for an extended period, assuming that they remain trusted throughout the session. This approach creates security gaps, as attackers who compromise credentials can exploit persistent access to move laterally within an organization's network. Continuous monitoring addresses this issue by continuously analyzing user behavior, device security posture, and network conditions to detect potential security threats. Instead of assuming that a user remains trustworthy after initial authentication, continuous monitoring evaluates trust dynamically, adapting access controls in real time based on changing risk factors.

Risk-based authentication enhances security by assessing contextual risk before granting or maintaining access. Instead of applying uniform authentication policies for all users, risk-based authentication evaluates the likelihood of an authentication request being fraudulent or compromised. Factors such as login location, device health, login frequency, and behavioral patterns contribute to a risk score, which determines whether additional authentication measures are required. If a user logs in from a familiar device and location, they may experience a frictionless authentication process. However, if the same user attempts to access critical systems from an unfamiliar device or a high-risk location, they may be prompted for multi-factor authentication (MFA) or additional verification steps.

Behavioral analytics plays a key role in continuous monitoring by detecting deviations from normal user behavior. Machine learning models analyze historical access patterns to establish baselines for typical user activity. If a user suddenly attempts to access resources they have never used before, downloads an unusually large volume of data, or exhibits login behavior inconsistent with their past activity, the system can flag the session as suspicious. In response, the organization can enforce adaptive security controls, such as requiring additional authentication, restricting access to certain resources, or terminating the session entirely. By leveraging behavioral analytics, organizations can detect insider threats, compromised accounts, and unauthorized privilege escalation attempts in real time.

Device security posture is another crucial factor in continuous monitoring and risk-based authentication. Organizations enforce security policies that evaluate whether a device meets predefined security standards before granting access. Factors such as operating system version, patch level, presence of antivirus software, and encryption status determine whether a device is compliant with security requirements. If a device is found to be out of compliance, access may be restricted, or the user may be required to remediate the security issue before proceeding. This approach ensures that only trusted and secure devices can connect to corporate resources, reducing the risk of malware infections and unauthorized access through compromised endpoints.

Network and session analysis contribute to dynamic access control by continuously assessing the security of active sessions. Instead of granting indefinite access once a session is established, organizations implement session monitoring to detect anomalies such as session hijacking, unusual IP address changes, and suspicious activities. If an authenticated session suddenly switches to a different IP address or is accessed from multiple locations simultaneously, the system can prompt for re-authentication or terminate the session to prevent account takeover attacks. This type of real-time risk assessment ensures that even authenticated users remain subject to ongoing security scrutiny throughout their session.

Adaptive authentication integrates with risk-based authentication to provide a seamless balance between security and user experience.

Organizations must ensure that security controls do not create excessive friction for legitimate users while still maintaining strong security policies. Adaptive authentication allows organizations to apply stronger authentication measures only when necessary. For example, a user accessing a corporate application from a trusted network and device may not be required to enter an additional MFA code. However, if the same user logs in from a new device or an unknown location, the system may enforce step-up authentication by requiring biometric verification, a hardware security key, or an out-of-band authentication method.

Zero Trust security frameworks align with continuous monitoring and risk-based authentication by eliminating implicit trust and enforcing dynamic access verification. In a Zero Trust model, users and devices must continuously prove their legitimacy before gaining or maintaining access to sensitive systems. This approach reduces the risk of security breaches by ensuring that even trusted users are subject to ongoing verification based on real-time risk assessments. Organizations implementing Zero Trust integrate continuous monitoring and risk-based authentication into their security architecture to ensure that access decisions are always based on the latest security intelligence.

Compliance and regulatory requirements drive the adoption of continuous monitoring and risk-based authentication in industries handling sensitive data. Regulations such as GDPR, HIPAA, and PCI DSS mandate strict access controls, identity verification, and security monitoring to protect personal and financial information. Organizations that fail to implement continuous monitoring risk falling out of compliance, exposing themselves to regulatory fines and reputational damage. By enforcing real-time authentication and continuously assessing risk, organizations strengthen their compliance posture while improving security.

Automation enhances continuous monitoring and risk-based authentication by reducing the need for manual intervention in security decision-making. AI-driven security solutions analyze access requests, detect anomalies, and apply security policies dynamically without human oversight. Automated response mechanisms ensure that high-risk authentication attempts are blocked, compromised sessions are terminated, and security alerts are generated in real time. This reduces the workload on security teams while ensuring that threats are addressed promptly. By integrating automation with IAM and security information and event management (SIEM) solutions, organizations create a more efficient and proactive security framework.

Organizations implementing continuous monitoring and risk-based authentication must balance security with usability. While strong authentication controls reduce security risks, overly aggressive policies can lead to user frustration and operational inefficiencies. Security teams must design authentication workflows that minimize friction while maintaining strong protection. By leveraging intelligent authentication mechanisms such as passwordless login, biometric authentication, and contextual MFA, organizations can improve security without negatively impacting user experience.

Continuous monitoring and risk-based authentication are essential for modern cybersecurity strategies, ensuring that access decisions are based on real-time risk assessments rather than static security policies. By continuously evaluating user behavior, device security, network conditions, and session activity, organizations can detect threats proactively and enforce adaptive security measures. Integrating machine learning, automation, and Zero Trust principles into these security controls enhances protection against evolving cyber threats while maintaining seamless and efficient access management.

The Importance of Identity Lifecycle Management

Identity Lifecycle Management (ILM) is a fundamental aspect of Identity and Access Management (IAM) that governs the creation, management, and deactivation of user identities throughout their lifecycle within an organization. Proper identity lifecycle management ensures that users receive the appropriate access to resources based on their roles and responsibilities while preventing unauthorized access and reducing security risks. As organizations grow and adopt hybrid work models, cloud services, and third-party integrations, managing user identities effectively becomes more complex and critical to maintaining security, compliance, and operational efficiency.

The identity lifecycle begins with identity creation, also known as user onboarding. When a new employee, contractor, or business partner joins an organization, their digital identity must be provisioned across multiple systems, applications, and services. This includes creating user accounts, assigning roles, and granting access to necessary resources. Automating this process through IAM solutions reduces administrative overhead, ensures consistency, and prevents delays in user access. Manual provisioning increases the risk of errors, such as assigning incorrect permissions or failing to create necessary accounts, which can lead to security vulnerabilities and productivity disruptions.

Role-based access control (RBAC) and attribute-based access control (ABAC) play a crucial role in identity provisioning. RBAC assigns permissions based on predefined roles within the organization, ensuring that users receive the appropriate level of access according to their job function. ABAC enhances this process by dynamically adjusting access based on attributes such as job title, department, location, and device security posture. By leveraging these access control models, organizations can enforce least privilege access, reducing the risk of excessive permissions and unauthorized data exposure.

Once a user's identity is provisioned, identity lifecycle management involves continuous monitoring and access adjustments as job roles evolve. Employees often change roles, move between departments, or take on temporary assignments that require different access levels. Without proper identity lifecycle management, users may accumulate unnecessary permissions over time, creating a security risk known as privilege creep. Regular access reviews and automated role adjustments ensure that users only retain the permissions they need for their current responsibilities. Implementing workflows for role transitions minimizes security gaps and ensures that permissions are updated in real time based on organizational changes.

Identity governance is an essential component of identity lifecycle management, ensuring that user access remains compliant with security policies and regulatory requirements. Organizations must conduct periodic access certifications, requiring managers and system owners to review and approve user access rights. Compliance regulations such as GDPR, HIPAA, and SOX mandate strict access controls, making it necessary to monitor and audit user permissions regularly. Identity lifecycle management solutions integrate access reviews with audit logs, providing visibility into user activities and ensuring that organizations can demonstrate compliance during security assessments.

Self-service identity management capabilities enhance efficiency while maintaining security. Employees should have the ability to request access to applications, reset passwords, and update personal information through self-service portals without requiring IT intervention. Automated approval workflows ensure that access requests are reviewed and granted based on predefined policies, reducing the administrative burden on IT teams while maintaining strict security controls. Self-service password reset functionality reduces helpdesk costs and minimizes downtime caused by forgotten credentials, improving the overall user experience.

Privileged access management (PAM) is closely related to identity lifecycle management, particularly for users with elevated privileges. System administrators, developers, and executives often require higher levels of access to perform critical tasks. However, standing privileged access poses a security risk, as compromised administrative accounts can lead to significant data breaches. Just-in-Time (JIT) access provisioning ensures that privileged users receive elevated permissions only for the duration necessary to complete specific tasks. Once the task is completed, the privileged access is revoked automatically, reducing the attack surface and mitigating the risk of insider threats or credential misuse.

Identity lifecycle management extends beyond human users to include machine identities, such as service accounts, APIs, and automated processes. As organizations increasingly rely on cloud services, DevOps pipelines, and IoT devices, the number of non-human identities continues to grow. These identities must be managed securely to prevent unauthorized access and data exposure. Identity lifecycle management solutions enforce security policies for machine identities, ensuring that service accounts follow the principle of least privilege and are deprovisioned when no longer needed. Secure API authentication, automated credential rotation, and continuous monitoring of machine identities reduce the risk of compromised service accounts being exploited by attackers.

Deprovisioning user access is one of the most critical stages of identity lifecycle management. When an employee leaves an organization, their access to corporate systems and data must be revoked immediately to prevent unauthorized access. Failure to deprovision accounts in a timely manner can lead to security risks, such as former employees retaining access to sensitive data or accounts being exploited by malicious actors. Automated deprovisioning ensures that all user accounts, credentials, and privileges are revoked as part of the offboarding process. Integrating IAM with HR systems enables real-time deprovisioning based on employment status changes, reducing the risk of orphaned accounts.

Identity lifecycle management solutions leverage automation, artificial intelligence, and analytics to enhance security and efficiency. AI-driven identity analytics detect anomalies in user access patterns, identifying excessive permissions, unused accounts, and suspicious activity. Automated remediation actions, such as revoking unnecessary access or enforcing additional authentication, ensure that security policies remain effective without manual intervention. Machine learning models continuously refine identity policies based on evolving risk factors, helping organizations proactively manage access and prevent security incidents.

Zero Trust security frameworks rely on strong identity lifecycle management to enforce continuous verification and dynamic access control. Zero Trust operates on the principle that no user or device should be inherently trusted, requiring identity verification at every access request. Identity lifecycle management ensures that users undergo authentication and authorization checks throughout their engagement with an organization, reducing the risk of unauthorized access. By integrating Zero Trust principles with identity governance, organizations can enforce real-time access decisions based on risk assessments, ensuring that security remains adaptive and responsive to changing conditions.

As cyber threats continue to evolve, identity lifecycle management plays an increasingly vital role in protecting enterprise resources, preventing data breaches, and maintaining compliance. By automating identity provisioning, enforcing least privilege access, conducting regular access reviews, and integrating AI-driven analytics, organizations can strengthen their security posture while improving operational efficiency. Identity lifecycle management is not just a security function; it is a strategic enabler that ensures users have the right access at the right time while preventing unauthorized activity and minimizing security risks.

Implementing Zero Trust in Cloud Environments

Zero Trust is a security framework designed to eliminate implicit trust and continuously verify every access request before granting permissions. As organizations migrate workloads to the cloud, the traditional perimeter-based security model becomes ineffective in protecting cloud resources. Cloud environments are highly dynamic, with users, applications, and devices accessing data from multiple locations, often beyond the control of corporate networks. Implementing Zero Trust in cloud environments ensures that security policies adapt to these evolving challenges by enforcing strong identity verification, least privilege access, continuous monitoring, and real-time risk assessment.

Cloud environments introduce new complexities in access control, as applications and services operate across multiple cloud providers and hybrid infrastructures. Unlike traditional on-premises systems, where access is managed within a single corporate perimeter, cloud environments require granular access policies that extend beyond network-based controls. Zero Trust shifts security from a network-centric approach to an identity- and data-centric model. Every access request in the cloud is authenticated, authorized, and continuously evaluated based on contextual risk factors, including user identity, device health, network conditions, and behavior anomalies.

Identity and Access Management (IAM) is the foundation of Zero Trust in cloud environments, ensuring that only verified users and devices can access cloud resources. Cloud IAM solutions, such as AWS IAM, Azure AD, and Google Cloud IAM, provide centralized control over identity authentication and authorization. Organizations implement multi-factor authentication (MFA) to enhance security, requiring users to provide additional verification beyond just a password. Passwordless authentication methods, including biometric authentication and FIDO2 security keys, further strengthen identity verification while reducing the risks associated with credential-based attacks.

Least privilege access is a key principle in implementing Zero Trust in the cloud, ensuring that users and applications receive only the minimum permissions necessary to perform their tasks. Cloud environments often suffer from overprivileged accounts, where users and service accounts have excessive access rights that can be exploited by attackers. Role-based access control (RBAC) and attribute-based access control (ABAC) enforce fine-grained permissions, dynamically adjusting access based on job roles, security attributes, and contextual risk factors. Organizations continuously review and refine access policies to eliminate unnecessary privileges and prevent privilege escalation attacks.

Micro-segmentation is an essential security strategy in Zero Trust cloud implementations, limiting lateral movement within cloud environments. Traditional network segmentation methods rely on perimeter defenses, which become less effective in cloud architectures where resources are distributed across multiple regions and providers. Micro-segmentation enforces security policies at the workload level, isolating applications, containers, and virtual machines from one another. This approach prevents attackers from moving laterally between cloud workloads if one component is compromised. Software-defined perimeters (SDP) further enhance security by creating logical access boundaries that restrict direct access to cloud resources based on identity and trust verification.

Zero Trust Network Access (ZTNA) replaces traditional VPNs, providing secure, identity-based access to cloud applications and services. Unlike VPNs, which grant broad network access once a user is authenticated, ZTNA enforces granular access controls, allowing users to connect only to specific applications based on predefined policies. Cloud-delivered ZTNA solutions integrate with IAM and endpoint security tools to ensure that access requests are continuously verified, and unauthorized connections are blocked. ZTNA reduces the attack surface by eliminating unnecessary network exposure, making it an essential component of Zero Trust in cloud environments.

Continuous monitoring and real-time threat detection enhance Zero Trust security in the cloud by identifying suspicious activity and potential breaches. Cloud environments generate vast amounts of access and usage data, requiring organizations to implement security analytics, machine learning, and behavioral monitoring to detect anomalies. Cloud-native security information and event management (SIEM) solutions analyze logs, access patterns, and system behaviors to identify potential security incidents. User and entity behavior analytics (UEBA) further strengthen security by detecting deviations from normal activity, such as unauthorized data transfers, abnormal login attempts, and privilege escalation.

Zero Trust in cloud environments requires strong endpoint security to prevent compromised devices from accessing cloud resources. Organizations implement endpoint detection and response (EDR) solutions to assess device health, enforce security policies, and detect malware threats before granting access. Conditional access policies evaluate device compliance, blocking or restricting access if a device does not meet security requirements. Integration with mobile device management (MDM) and endpoint protection platforms ensures that corporate security policies extend to mobile devices, laptops, and IoT endpoints accessing cloud applications.

Data protection and encryption play a crucial role in securing sensitive information in cloud environments. Zero Trust enforces data-centric security, ensuring that access to data is controlled based on identity, device, and location. Cloud providers offer encryption services that protect data at rest, in transit, and during processing. Organizations implement data loss prevention (DLP) policies to prevent unauthorized data sharing and enforce strict access controls for sensitive information. Digital rights management (DRM) technologies further enhance security by restricting how data can be accessed and shared, even after it has been downloaded or transferred outside the corporate environment.

Cloud security posture management (CSPM) helps organizations maintain compliance with security best practices and regulatory requirements in cloud environments. CSPM tools continuously scan cloud configurations, detecting misconfigurations, excessive permissions, and policy violations that could expose data to unauthorized access. Compliance frameworks such as GDPR, HIPAA, and SOC 2 require organizations to implement strict access controls and continuous monitoring, making Zero Trust a necessary approach for achieving regulatory compliance. Automated security assessments and compliance reporting streamline governance, reducing the risk of cloud security misconfigurations.

Automation and artificial intelligence enhance Zero Trust security in cloud environments by reducing manual security operations and enabling rapid threat response. AI-driven identity analytics detect anomalous access patterns, flagging potential security threats before they escalate. Automated remediation workflows enforce access control policies in real time, revoking permissions or triggering incident response actions when security risks are detected. Cloud-native security automation tools integrate with IAM, SIEM, and endpoint security solutions to provide a seamless and proactive Zero Trust security framework.

Implementing Zero Trust in cloud environments requires a holistic security strategy that integrates IAM, least privilege access, micro-segmentation, ZTNA, continuous monitoring, and data protection. As organizations continue to embrace cloud computing, hybrid workforces, and multi-cloud architectures, Zero Trust provides a scalable and adaptive security model that protects cloud workloads, applications, and data from evolving cyber threats. By enforcing identity-centric security controls and continuously verifying trust, organizations can reduce the attack surface, mitigate security risks, and ensure secure access to cloud resources.

Micro-Segmentation and IAM Security

Micro-segmentation is a security strategy that divides networks into smaller, isolated segments to minimize unauthorized access and restrict lateral movement within an environment. It is a key component of modern cybersecurity frameworks, particularly in Zero Trust and Identity and Access Management (IAM) security models. By enforcing strict access controls at a granular level, micro-segmentation ensures that users, devices, and applications can only communicate with authorized resources. This approach reduces the risk of data breaches, limits the spread of malware, and enhances overall security posture by restricting unnecessary access to critical assets.

Traditional network security models relied on perimeter-based defenses, assuming that threats originated from outside the corporate network while internal systems were inherently trusted. However, this approach has proven inadequate in today's dynamic IT environments, where cloud computing, remote work, and hybrid infrastructures have eliminated clear network boundaries. Once an attacker breaches the perimeter, they can move laterally through interconnected systems, exploiting weak access controls to escalate privileges and compromise sensitive data. Micro-segmentation addresses this issue by creating internal barriers that enforce strict identity-based access controls, ensuring that even authenticated users and devices cannot access unauthorized systems.

IAM plays a crucial role in micro-segmentation by managing and enforcing access policies based on user identity, role, and contextual risk factors. Unlike traditional network segmentation, which relies on static IP addresses and firewall rules, IAM-driven micro-segmentation dynamically adjusts access permissions based on real-time authentication and authorization decisions. This means that access to specific workloads, applications, or databases is granted based on identity attributes rather than network location. By integrating IAM with micro-segmentation, organizations can enforce least privilege access and prevent unauthorized lateral movement, even if an attacker gains access to a legitimate user account.

One of the key benefits of micro-segmentation in IAM security is its ability to enforce identity-aware access policies. Instead of relying solely on network-based controls, micro-segmentation ensures that access is granted based on user roles, job functions, and security posture. For example, a finance department employee may have access to financial databases but should not be able to interact with IT infrastructure components. Similarly, a developer may be allowed to deploy code in a test environment but restricted from accessing production servers. By aligning access policies with user identities, micro-segmentation reduces the risk of unauthorized access and privilege misuse.

Micro-segmentation enhances security in cloud environments, where traditional perimeter-based security measures are ineffective. Cloud workloads, containers, and virtual machines are highly dynamic, frequently changing states and interacting with multiple services across different cloud providers. Static access control lists (ACLs) and firewall rules cannot effectively manage these dynamic interactions. IAM-integrated micro-segmentation ensures that access to cloud workloads is controlled based on identity authentication, device trust, and contextual risk factors. This approach prevents unauthorized service-to-service communication and reduces the attack surface in multi-cloud and hybrid cloud deployments.

Zero Trust Network Access (ZTNA) and micro-segmentation work together to enforce strict access control policies. ZTNA ensures that users and devices undergo continuous authentication and authorization before accessing applications, while micro-segmentation restricts access within the network based on IAM policies. Unlike traditional VPNs, which grant broad network access once authenticated, ZTNA combined with micro-segmentation enforces granular access controls, allowing users to connect only to authorized applications and services. This eliminates the risk of lateral movement and ensures that even if an attacker compromises a user account, their ability to access critical systems remains limited.

Privileged Access Management (PAM) and micro-segmentation further strengthen IAM security by controlling access to high-value assets and administrative functions. Privileged accounts, such as system administrators and database managers, require elevated permissions that, if compromised, could lead to catastrophic security breaches. PAM solutions enforce just-in-time (JIT) access, ensuring that privileged users receive temporary permissions for specific tasks rather than maintaining standing access. When combined with micro-segmentation, PAM policies restrict privileged users to designated network segments, preventing unauthorized interactions between sensitive systems. This minimizes the risk of privilege escalation and insider threats.

Behavioral analytics and continuous monitoring enhance micro-segmentation by identifying abnormal access patterns and enforcing dynamic security policies. IAM-integrated security solutions analyze user behavior to detect deviations from normal activity. If a user suddenly attempts to access a restricted segment or exhibits unusual login behavior, the system can trigger additional authentication challenges, revoke access, or isolate the user from critical resources. This real-time security enforcement ensures that access policies remain adaptive and responsive to emerging threats.

Micro-segmentation also improves security for machine identities, including service accounts, APIs, and automated processes. As organizations rely more on automation and cloud-native applications, the number of machine-to-machine interactions continues to grow. These interactions must be secured using IAM-based policies that regulate how services communicate. Micro-segmentation ensures that service accounts can only interact with predefined resources, preventing unauthorized API calls and restricting access to sensitive data. By securing machine identities with micro-segmentation, organizations reduce the risk of automated attacks and API abuse.

Compliance and regulatory requirements further drive the adoption of micro-segmentation in IAM security. Regulations such as GDPR, HIPAA, and PCI DSS mandate strict access controls, data protection measures, and network segmentation to prevent unauthorized access to sensitive information. Micro-segmentation helps organizations achieve compliance by enforcing identity-based access policies, logging all access attempts, and preventing unauthorized data transfers. Security teams can use IAM-integrated micro-segmentation to create audit trails, demonstrating compliance with regulatory standards while improving overall security governance.

Implementing micro-segmentation in IAM security requires a combination of policy enforcement, automation, and real-time monitoring. Organizations must define clear access control policies based on identity attributes, ensuring that users and devices can only access authorized resources. Automation streamlines the segmentation process by dynamically adjusting access permissions based on risk assessments and behavioral analytics. Continuous monitoring ensures that access policies remain effective, detecting and responding to security threats before they escalate. By integrating micro-segmentation with IAM solutions, organizations can create a scalable and adaptive security framework that protects critical assets while enabling secure and efficient operations.

Micro-segmentation is a powerful security strategy that enhances IAM by enforcing strict access controls, preventing unauthorized lateral movement, and reducing the attack surface in complex IT environments. By integrating identity-aware access policies with micro-segmentation, organizations can strengthen Zero Trust security, secure cloud workloads, protect privileged accounts, and comply with regulatory requirements. As cyber threats evolve, micro-segmentation remains a critical component of modern cybersecurity strategies, ensuring that access to sensitive systems and data is continuously verified and restricted based on identity and risk assessment.

Threat Intelligence and IAM Decision Making

Threat intelligence plays a critical role in modern Identity and Access Management (IAM) decision-making by providing real-time insights into potential security threats, compromised credentials, and emerging attack patterns. As cyber threats become more sophisticated, organizations can no longer rely on static access controls and predefined policies to protect their systems and data. Instead, IAM must integrate with threat intelligence platforms to dynamically assess risks, adjust access policies, and prevent unauthorized access based on the latest security insights. By leveraging threat intelligence, organizations can make informed IAM decisions that enhance security, improve detection capabilities, and reduce the risk of identity-based attacks.

IAM traditionally focuses on authenticating users and authorizing access based on predefined rules. However, these rules do not always account for evolving threats, compromised credentials, or changes in attack tactics. Threat intelligence enhances IAM by providing contextual awareness of potential risks before granting access. For example, if an IAM system detects that a user's credentials have been exposed in a data breach, it can enforce additional authentication measures, such as multi-factor authentication (MFA), or immediately revoke access until the account is secured. This proactive approach prevents attackers from using stolen credentials to gain unauthorized access.

External threat intelligence sources, such as dark web monitoring services and cybersecurity threat feeds, provide organizations with valuable data on compromised credentials, phishing campaigns, and known attack indicators. By integrating this intelligence with IAM systems, organizations can automatically detect when a user's credentials appear in leaked databases or if their account exhibits suspicious activity. If an IAM system identifies that a user's email and password combination has been leaked in a breach, it can trigger an automatic password reset, notify the user, or block access until identity verification is completed. This reduces the risk of credential stuffing attacks, where attackers use leaked credentials to attempt unauthorized logins.

Threat intelligence also enhances risk-based authentication by dynamically adjusting security measures based on real-time threat assessments. Instead of applying uniform authentication policies for all users, IAM can use threat intelligence to determine risk levels and enforce appropriate security controls. For instance, if a login attempt originates from a country known for cybercriminal activity or from an IP address associated with botnet traffic, the IAM system can require step-up authentication, such as biometric verification or a security key challenge. This ensures that users accessing sensitive systems undergo stricter authentication checks when potential threats are detected.

User behavior analytics (UBA) combined with threat intelligence improves IAM decision-making by identifying anomalies in user activity. Traditional access control models grant permissions based on static roles, assuming that users will always behave predictably. However, attackers who compromise an account may attempt to escalate privileges, access unusual data, or perform unauthorized actions. By analyzing login patterns, resource access history, and behavioral deviations, IAM systems can detect suspicious activity and respond in real time. If a user suddenly attempts to download large amounts of sensitive data, accesses resources outside their normal job function, or logs in from multiple locations within a short time frame, the system can flag the behavior as a potential threat and take corrective actions.

Threat intelligence helps organizations enforce least privilege access by continuously evaluating risk and refining access policies. Many organizations struggle with excessive permissions, where users retain access to systems and data they no longer need. Attackers often exploit overprivileged accounts to move laterally within a network, gaining access to critical resources. By integrating threat intelligence with IAM, organizations can conduct automated access reviews, identifying accounts with unnecessary privileges and revoking access based on risk assessments. If an account shows signs of being compromised or is linked to external threat intelligence indicators, IAM can enforce stricter access controls or require reauthorization.

Cloud environments introduce additional IAM challenges, as users, applications, and services interact across multiple platforms. Threat intelligence provides cloud IAM solutions with insights into emerging attack vectors, enabling organizations to enforce adaptive access controls based on evolving threats. Cloud identity providers, such as AWS IAM, Azure AD, and Google Cloud IAM, integrate with threat intelligence platforms to assess login risks, detect compromised accounts, and enforce security policies in real time. For example, if a cloud administrator's account is flagged in an external threat feed as compromised, IAM can trigger an automated access review, suspend privileged access, or enforce just-in-time (JIT) access provisioning to prevent unauthorized actions.

Privileged Access Management (PAM) benefits significantly from threat intelligence, as privileged accounts are prime targets for attackers. Threat intelligence allows organizations to monitor threat actors targeting administrative accounts and enforce stricter security controls. If intelligence feeds detect an increase in attacks against privileged credentials, PAM solutions can enforce additional authentication layers, restrict access to critical systems, or require approvals for high-risk actions. By leveraging real-time threat intelligence, organizations can proactively secure privileged accounts before they become compromised.

Threat intelligence also supports Zero Trust security models by continuously validating trust before granting access. Zero Trust assumes that no user, device, or application should be inherently trusted, requiring continuous authentication and authorization based on contextual risk. Threat intelligence enhances this model by identifying external risks, assessing trust levels dynamically, and ensuring that access decisions are based on real-time security insights. If a user's identity is linked to known cyber threats or suspicious activities, Zero Trust policies can restrict access until further verification is performed.

Automation and artificial intelligence (AI) further enhance the integration of threat intelligence with IAM decision-making. AI-driven security analytics process large volumes of threat data, identifying patterns and correlating them with IAM policies to improve security responses. Automated remediation actions, such as disabling compromised accounts, resetting passwords, or enforcing step-up authentication, help security teams respond to threats in real time. Machine learning models continuously refine access control policies based on threat intelligence data, ensuring that IAM remains adaptive and resilient against evolving attack tactics.

Compliance and regulatory requirements increasingly emphasize the need for proactive security measures, making threat intelligence an essential component of IAM governance. Regulations such as GDPR, HIPAA, and PCI DSS require organizations to monitor access controls, detect unauthorized access attempts, and protect user identities from cyber threats. Threat intelligence provides organizations with the tools to meet these compliance requirements by ensuring that IAM policies are continuously updated based on emerging security risks. By incorporating threat intelligence into IAM decision-making, organizations strengthen their compliance posture while reducing the risk of identity-related breaches.

Threat intelligence transforms IAM from a static access management system into a dynamic and proactive security framework. By leveraging real-time threat data, behavioral analytics, and risk-based authentication, organizations can improve access control decisions, prevent unauthorized access, and enhance overall security. Integrating threat intelligence with IAM ensures that access policies remain aligned with the evolving threat landscape, enabling organizations to detect, respond to, and mitigate security risks before they escalate.

Zero Trust and Insider Threat Protection

Zero Trust is a security framework designed to eliminate implicit trust and continuously verify every access request based on identity, behavior, and risk. While traditional security models focus on external threats, insider threats pose an equally significant risk to organizations. Employees, contractors, and business partners often have legitimate access to critical systems and data, making it difficult to detect and prevent malicious or negligent actions. Zero Trust enhances insider threat protection by enforcing strict access controls, monitoring user activity, and applying risk-based authentication to ensure that no user is granted unnecessary or excessive privileges.

Insider threats can originate from malicious actors within an organization who intentionally abuse their access to steal data, sabotage systems, or engage in fraudulent activities. However, insider threats also include negligent users who inadvertently expose sensitive information through poor security practices, such as sharing passwords, falling victim to phishing attacks, or misconfiguring access controls. Zero Trust mitigates these risks by assuming that all users and devices could be potential threats, requiring continuous verification before granting or maintaining access to resources.

Identity and Access Management (IAM) plays a central role in Zero Trust by ensuring that every user is authenticated, authorized, and continuously monitored. Traditional IAM models rely on static permissions, where users receive access based on predefined roles. This approach often leads to privilege creep, where employees accumulate unnecessary access over time, increasing the risk of insider threats. Zero Trust enforces least privilege access by dynamically adjusting permissions based on real-time risk assessments, ensuring that users only have access to the data and applications necessary for their roles.

Behavioral analytics and user activity monitoring are essential components of Zero Trust for insider threat detection. Organizations analyze user behavior to identify anomalies that may indicate malicious intent or compromised credentials. If an employee who typically accesses financial reports suddenly attempts to download large amounts of customer data, the system can flag this behavior as suspicious and trigger additional authentication measures, restrict access, or alert security teams. Continuous monitoring ensures that even authenticated users remain subject to security scrutiny, reducing the likelihood of insider threats going undetected.

Multi-Factor Authentication (MFA) enhances insider threat protection by requiring users to verify their identity through multiple factors before accessing critical systems. Passwords alone are insufficient in preventing insider threats, as they can be easily shared, stolen, or compromised. By enforcing MFA, organizations add an additional layer of security that reduces the risk of unauthorized access, even if login credentials are compromised. Adaptive authentication further strengthens security by adjusting authentication requirements based on user behavior, device security posture, and access location. If a user attempts to log in from an unrecognized device or an unusual location, the system can require biometric authentication or additional verification before granting access.

Privileged Access Management (PAM) is a critical component of Zero Trust that protects against insider threats by controlling and monitoring privileged accounts. Administrative users, system administrators, and executives often have elevated access to critical infrastructure, making them prime targets for insider attacks. PAM solutions enforce just-in-time (JIT) access, granting temporary privileges only when needed and revoking them after the task is completed. This prevents users from maintaining standing administrative access, reducing the risk of privilege misuse or exploitation by attackers. Additionally, PAM solutions log and monitor all privileged activities, providing security teams with visibility into high-risk actions.

Micro-segmentation enhances insider threat protection by limiting lateral movement within an organization's network. Traditional network security models allow users with access to one system to move freely between connected resources, increasing the potential damage an insider threat can cause. Zero Trust enforces micro-segmentation by isolating workloads, applications, and databases, ensuring that users can only access the specific resources necessary for their tasks. Even if an insider attempts to escalate privileges or access unauthorized data, micro-segmentation restricts their ability to move laterally, preventing widespread damage.

Data Loss Prevention (DLP) solutions integrate with Zero Trust to prevent insiders from exfiltrating sensitive information. Organizations define policies that monitor and control data transfers, blocking unauthorized sharing of confidential files via email, cloud storage, or external devices. If an insider attempts to copy sensitive data to a USB drive or upload files to an unapproved cloud service, the system can block the action and generate an alert for security teams. DLP solutions also enforce encryption policies, ensuring that sensitive data remains protected even if it is accessed by unauthorized users.

Zero Trust extends insider threat protection to third-party users and contractors who require access to enterprise systems. External vendors and business partners often need temporary access to applications, but granting them long-term credentials increases security risks. Zero Trust enforces strict access policies for third parties by requiring just-in-time access provisioning, limiting permissions to only necessary systems, and continuously monitoring their activity. Organizations also implement Zero Trust Network Access (ZTNA) to ensure that third-party users do not gain broad network access, instead restricting them to specific applications based on identity and security posture.

Cloud environments introduce additional risks for insider threats, as users access resources from multiple locations and devices. Zero Trust strengthens cloud security by continuously verifying user and device trust before granting access. Cloud IAM solutions enforce conditional access policies, requiring users to authenticate with strong security controls before accessing sensitive cloud workloads. Organizations also implement cloud security posture management (CSPM) to detect and remediate misconfigurations that could expose data to insider threats. By applying Zero Trust principles to cloud access, organizations ensure that insider threats are minimized across distributed IT environments.

Artificial intelligence (AI) and machine learning enhance insider threat protection by identifying patterns of suspicious activity and automating threat response. AI-driven security analytics analyze vast amounts of user behavior data to detect anomalies that may indicate an insider threat. Automated threat detection systems can respond in real time by revoking access, triggering security alerts, or requiring additional verification before allowing potentially risky actions. By leveraging AI for threat detection, organizations reduce the time it takes to identify and mitigate insider threats, preventing data breaches before they escalate.

Regulatory compliance frameworks, including GDPR, HIPAA, and PCI DSS, require organizations to implement strict access controls and monitor user activity to prevent unauthorized access. Zero Trust aligns with these compliance requirements by enforcing continuous authentication, least privilege access, and comprehensive logging of all user interactions. Security teams use IAM audit logs and forensic analysis tools to track insider activities, ensuring that all access decisions are transparent and auditable. By integrating Zero Trust with compliance strategies, organizations not only enhance security but also reduce regulatory risks associated with insider threats.

Zero Trust provides a proactive approach to insider threat protection by continuously verifying trust, enforcing least privilege access, monitoring user behavior, and restricting unauthorized lateral movement. As organizations face increasing threats from malicious insiders, negligent employees, and compromised accounts, implementing Zero Trust ensures that security remains adaptive, identity-centric, and resilient against internal risks. By leveraging IAM, PAM, micro-segmentation, AI-driven analytics, and real-time monitoring, organizations can effectively mitigate insider threats while maintaining a secure and efficient operational environment.

Automating IAM with AI and Machine Learning

Artificial intelligence (AI) and machine learning (ML) are transforming Identity and Access Management (IAM) by enabling automation, adaptive security, and intelligent decision-making. Traditional IAM systems rely on static policies and manual processes, which can be slow, error-prone, and difficult to scale. As organizations grow and adopt cloud-based environments, managing identities, permissions, and authentication manually becomes increasingly complex. AI and ML enhance IAM by automating identity governance, detecting anomalies, enforcing risk-based authentication, and continuously adapting access controls based on real-time behavioral analysis.

IAM automation begins with identity lifecycle management, which governs how user identities are created, modified, and deprovisioned. AI-driven IAM solutions streamline the onboarding and offboarding process by automatically assigning roles, provisioning access, and revoking permissions when users leave the organization. Machine learning algorithms analyze patterns in user access requests, detecting inconsistencies and suggesting optimal role assignments based on historical data. By automating these processes, organizations reduce administrative overhead, prevent privilege creep, and ensure that users have the right level of access at all times.

Role-Based Access Control (RBAC) and Attribute-Based Access Control (ABAC) benefit from AI-powered automation, allowing organizations to refine access policies dynamically. Traditional RBAC models require administrators to define and manage roles manually, often leading to role explosion, where too many overlapping roles create complexity and security risks. AI analyzes user behavior, job functions, and access patterns to recommend role adjustments, consolidating redundant roles and ensuring that users receive only necessary permissions. ABAC further enhances security by dynamically adjusting access based on real-time attributes, such as user location, device trust, and risk level. AI continuously refines these policies, ensuring that access control remains adaptive and efficient.

Risk-based authentication is a key area where AI and ML significantly improve IAM security. Static authentication methods apply the same security requirements to all users, regardless of risk level. AI-driven risk assessment dynamically adjusts authentication requirements based on contextual factors such as login location, device security posture, and behavioral anomalies. If a user logs in from a familiar device and location, access may be granted with minimal friction. However, if an authentication attempt originates from a high-risk country or an unusual device, the system may require additional verification through multi-factor authentication (MFA), biometric authentication, or one-time passcodes. By continuously analyzing risk factors, AI enhances security while improving user experience by reducing unnecessary authentication challenges.

User behavior analytics (UBA) powered by machine learning enhances IAM by detecting deviations from normal access patterns. Traditional security models rely on predefined rules to identify suspicious activity, but these rules often fail to detect new or sophisticated attacks. AI-driven UBA learns from historical user behavior, identifying anomalies such as unusual login times, access to unfamiliar resources, or rapid privilege escalation. If an employee suddenly attempts to download large amounts of sensitive data or access systems unrelated to their role, AI can trigger automated responses, such as alerting security teams, requiring additional authentication, or temporarily suspending access. This proactive approach helps prevent insider threats, account compromise, and privilege misuse.

Privileged Access Management (PAM) benefits from AI and ML by reducing the risk associated with administrative accounts. Privileged users have elevated access to critical systems, making them prime targets for cyberattacks. AI-driven PAM solutions enforce just-in-time (JIT) access, granting temporary privileges only when necessary and revoking them automatically after the task is completed. Machine learning algorithms analyze privileged user behavior, detecting suspicious activities such as unauthorized privilege escalation or attempts to bypass security controls. By continuously monitoring and adjusting privileged access policies, AI ensures that administrative accounts remain secure and compliant with least privilege principles.

Automated access reviews powered by AI improve compliance and governance in IAM. Traditional access certification processes require managers and IT administrators to manually review user permissions, which is time-consuming and prone to oversight. AI automates access reviews by analyzing user activity, identifying unused permissions, and recommending revocations for unnecessary access. Instead of reviewing thousands of access requests manually, security teams receive AI-generated reports highlighting high-risk accounts, excessive privileges, and anomalies. This automation accelerates compliance processes, reduces audit fatigue, and ensures that organizations adhere to security frameworks such as GDPR, HIPAA, and SOX.

Identity threat detection and response (ITDR) is another area where AI and ML improve IAM security. Attackers frequently target IAM systems through credential theft, phishing, and brute-force attacks. AI-driven threat detection analyzes authentication logs, network traffic, and user interactions to identify potential security threats. If an account exhibits signs of compromise—such as repeated failed login attempts, access from multiple geographic locations, or interactions with high-risk systems—the system can automatically trigger incident response actions. AI-driven IAM solutions integrate with security information and event management (SIEM) platforms to correlate identity-based threats with broader security events, providing a comprehensive defense against cyberattacks.

AI and ML also enhance fraud prevention in IAM, particularly in financial services and e-commerce environments. Fraudulent transactions and account takeovers often involve subtle behavior changes that traditional security rules fail to detect. AI models analyze transaction data, purchase history, and authentication patterns to identify fraudulent activities in real time. If a banking system detects an unusual withdrawal request from an account that has never conducted such a transaction, AI can trigger additional verification steps before processing the request. This adaptive fraud prevention approach minimizes false positives while effectively identifying and blocking fraudulent activities.

Cloud IAM automation powered by AI ensures that access controls remain consistent across multi-cloud and hybrid environments. Cloud security misconfigurations are a leading cause of data breaches, as organizations struggle to manage IAM policies across different platforms. AI-driven cloud security posture management (CSPM) continuously scans cloud environments, detecting misconfigurations, excessive permissions, and compliance violations. Automated remediation actions adjust access controls, enforce least privilege principles, and eliminate security risks without manual intervention. AI also assists in cloud identity federation, streamlining authentication processes across multiple cloud providers while maintaining strong security policies.

Zero Trust architectures rely on AI-driven IAM automation to enforce continuous verification and adaptive access control. Traditional perimeter-based security models grant implicit trust to authenticated users, but Zero Trust requires ongoing authentication and real-time risk assessment. AI automates trust evaluation by continuously analyzing user behavior, device security, and contextual risk factors. If an authenticated session deviates from normal activity patterns, AI can dynamically adjust access permissions, enforce additional security controls, or terminate the session to prevent potential threats. This continuous adaptation ensures that Zero Trust IAM remains effective in detecting and mitigating evolving cyber risks.

Organizations implementing AI-driven IAM automation must balance security with user experience. Overly restrictive access controls can hinder productivity, leading to frustration among employees and customers. AI helps optimize IAM workflows by intelligently managing access requests, reducing authentication friction, and providing self-service identity management capabilities. Machine learning models refine access policies over time, ensuring that security controls adapt to user needs while maintaining strong protection against unauthorized access.

AI and machine learning are transforming IAM by automating identity lifecycle management, enforcing risk-based authentication, detecting threats, and optimizing access governance. As organizations continue to adopt cloud computing, Zero Trust security models, and advanced authentication technologies, AI-driven IAM automation provides a scalable and intelligent approach to securing digital identities. By integrating AI into IAM decision-making, organizations enhance security, improve operational efficiency, and proactively defend against evolving cyber threats.

Implementing Zero Trust in Hybrid IT Environments

Zero Trust is a security framework that eliminates implicit trust and enforces continuous verification of users, devices, and applications before granting access to resources. In a hybrid IT environment, where organizations operate a mix of on-premises infrastructure, private clouds, and public cloud services, implementing Zero Trust presents unique challenges. Traditional perimeter-based security models are ineffective in these distributed environments, as users access corporate resources from multiple locations and through various networks. Zero Trust ensures that security policies adapt dynamically, verifying identity, device compliance, and risk factors at every access request.

Hybrid IT environments create security complexities due to the integration of legacy systems with cloud-based applications. Many organizations rely on on-premises Active Directory (AD) for identity management while simultaneously adopting cloud identity providers such as Azure Active Directory, AWS IAM, and Google Cloud Identity. Zero Trust requires a unified approach to identity and access management (IAM), where authentication and authorization policies remain consistent across all platforms. Organizations implement identity federation to enable seamless authentication between on-premises and cloud environments, ensuring that users can securely access resources without relying on outdated perimeter defenses.

Multi-Factor Authentication (MFA) is a foundational component of Zero Trust in hybrid IT environments, providing an additional layer of security beyond passwords. Legacy systems often lack built-in support for modern authentication mechanisms, making it necessary to integrate MFA solutions that extend across both on-premises and cloud applications. Adaptive authentication enhances security by analyzing contextual factors such as user location, device security posture, and behavioral anomalies before granting access. If a login attempt originates from an untrusted location or a compromised device, the system can enforce step-up authentication or block access entirely.

Least privilege access is essential in Zero Trust implementations, ensuring that users and applications only have the permissions necessary to perform their tasks. Hybrid IT environments often suffer from excessive permissions, where users accumulate access rights over time due to role changes, project assignments, or manual misconfigurations. Role-Based Access Control (RBAC) and Attribute-Based Access Control (ABAC) enforce strict access policies, dynamically adjusting permissions based on identity attributes, job roles, and security context. Continuous access reviews help organizations detect privilege creep, revoking unnecessary permissions and reducing the risk of insider threats.

Zero Trust Network Access (ZTNA) replaces traditional VPNs, providing secure access to applications and services in hybrid IT environments. VPNs grant broad network access once a user is authenticated, increasing the risk of lateral movement if credentials are compromised. ZTNA enforces granular access controls, ensuring that users can only connect to specific applications based on real-time identity verification and device compliance. Cloud-delivered ZTNA solutions integrate with IAM platforms, enabling organizations to enforce identity-aware access policies while eliminating unnecessary network exposure.

Micro-segmentation enhances Zero Trust by restricting lateral movement within hybrid IT environments. Traditional network security models allow users with access to one system to navigate freely across connected resources, increasing the potential impact of security breaches. Micro-segmentation isolates workloads, databases, and applications, ensuring that users can only interact with predefined resources based on IAM policies. If an attacker compromises an endpoint, micro-segmentation prevents them from moving laterally and accessing sensitive systems. Software-defined networking (SDN) and identity-aware firewalls further refine access policies, dynamically adjusting network segmentation based on security posture and risk assessments.

Privileged Access Management (PAM) is a critical component of Zero Trust in hybrid IT environments, controlling administrative access to critical infrastructure. System administrators, cloud engineers, and DevOps teams require elevated privileges to manage both on-premises and cloud-based resources. However, standing privileged access creates security risks, as compromised admin accounts can be used to escalate attacks. PAM solutions enforce just-in-time (JIT) access, granting temporary privileges only when needed and revoking them automatically after the session ends. Session monitoring and logging provide visibility into privileged activities, ensuring that all administrative actions are auditable and compliant with security policies.

Continuous monitoring and real-time threat detection strengthen Zero Trust security in hybrid IT environments by identifying suspicious behavior and potential breaches. Traditional security models rely on periodic audits and reactive incident response, leaving organizations vulnerable to undetected threats. Zero Trust integrates with Security

Information and Event Management (SIEM) platforms, User and Entity Behavior Analytics (UEBA), and Endpoint Detection and Response (EDR) solutions to continuously analyze user activity, detect anomalies, and respond to security incidents in real time. If an authenticated user suddenly exhibits unusual access patterns, such as downloading large amounts of sensitive data or attempting to access restricted systems, Zero Trust policies can trigger automated security responses.

Cloud security posture management (CSPM) helps organizations maintain compliance and enforce Zero Trust security policies across hybrid environments. Misconfigurations in cloud security settings are a leading cause of data breaches, as many organizations struggle to manage IAM policies consistently across multiple cloud platforms. CSPM solutions continuously scan cloud environments for security vulnerabilities, excessive permissions, and non-compliant access policies. Automated remediation ensures that security gaps are closed immediately, enforcing Zero Trust principles while maintaining compliance with industry regulations such as GDPR, HIPAA, and PCI DSS.

Endpoint security plays a crucial role in Zero Trust for hybrid IT environments, ensuring that only compliant and secure devices can access corporate resources. Organizations enforce device trust policies, assessing factors such as operating system version, encryption status, and security software compliance before granting access. If a device fails to meet security requirements, Zero Trust policies can restrict access or require remediation before allowing connections. Endpoint Detection and Response (EDR) solutions integrate with IAM to provide continuous visibility into device security posture, detecting and mitigating threats before they compromise critical systems.

Automation and artificial intelligence enhance Zero Trust security by dynamically adapting IAM policies based on evolving risk conditions. AI-driven IAM solutions analyze access requests, user behavior, and threat intelligence to enforce real-time security controls. Automated identity analytics detect excessive permissions, suspicious activity, and privilege misuse, enabling organizations to take proactive security measures. Machine learning models refine access policies over time, ensuring that Zero Trust implementations remain adaptive and responsive to emerging cyber threats.

Zero Trust governance ensures that IAM policies, security controls, and compliance requirements are consistently enforced across hybrid IT environments. Organizations implement centralized IAM frameworks that integrate with cloud identity providers, on-premises directory services, and third-party applications. Zero Trust governance includes automated access certifications, policy enforcement mechanisms, and security audits to maintain a continuous security posture. By standardizing IAM practices across all IT environments, organizations reduce security gaps and prevent identity-based attacks.

Zero Trust provides a scalable and adaptive security framework for hybrid IT environments, ensuring that access decisions are continuously verified based on identity, risk, and contextual awareness. By implementing strong authentication, least privilege access, micro-segmentation, ZTNA, and continuous monitoring, organizations protect both on-premises and cloud resources from cyber threats. As enterprises continue to adopt hybrid IT architectures, Zero Trust remains a critical security model for enforcing identity-centric security policies, reducing attack surfaces, and preventing unauthorized access across distributed environments.

The Role of Identity Federation in Zero Trust

Identity Federation is a key enabler of Zero Trust security, allowing organizations to manage authentication and access control across multiple domains, applications, and environments without relying on traditional perimeter-based security models. As enterprises adopt cloud computing, hybrid IT architectures, and Software-as-a-Service (SaaS) applications, the need for a unified and secure identity management framework becomes critical. Identity Federation ensures that users can access resources across different platforms using a single identity while maintaining strong authentication and authorization policies in line with Zero Trust principles.

Zero Trust security models assume that no user, device, or system should be trusted by default, requiring continuous authentication and authorization before granting access to resources. Traditional identity management approaches rely on isolated directories and identity silos, where users must authenticate separately for each system. This fragmentation increases security risks, creates inefficiencies, and complicates access management. Identity Federation addresses these challenges by allowing organizations to establish trust relationships between identity providers (IdPs) and service providers (SPs), enabling seamless and secure authentication across multiple platforms.

Federated identity management enables Single Sign-On (SSO), allowing users to authenticate once and gain access to multiple applications and services without repeatedly entering credentials. SSO reduces the risk of password fatigue, where users create weak or reused passwords due to managing multiple accounts. In a Zero Trust framework, SSO integrates with Multi-Factor Authentication (MFA) and risk-based authentication to enhance security. If a user's risk level is high due to unusual login behavior or a change in device security posture, the system can enforce additional authentication challenges before granting access. This dynamic approach strengthens authentication while improving the user experience.

Identity Federation relies on industry-standard protocols such as Security Assertion Markup Language (SAML), OpenID Connect (OIDC), and OAuth 2.0 to enable secure authentication and authorization across different environments. These protocols facilitate the exchange of identity attributes between identity providers and relying parties, ensuring that authentication decisions are made based on verified credentials and real-time security assessments. In a Zero Trust architecture, federated authentication ensures that access decisions are based on identity attributes, device trust, and contextual risk rather than static credentials or network location.

Zero Trust requires continuous validation of user identity, even after initial authentication. Federated identity solutions integrate with Zero Trust Network Access (ZTNA) frameworks, ensuring that authentication is not just a one-time event but an ongoing process. Unlike traditional VPNs, which grant broad network access once a user is authenticated, ZTNA enforces granular access controls based on user identity, device health, and real-time security posture. Identity Federation supports ZTNA by enabling centralized authentication across cloud applications, on-premises systems, and third-party services while ensuring that access is continuously evaluated.

Privileged Access Management (PAM) benefits from Identity Federation by centralizing authentication for privileged users while enforcing strict security controls. Administrative accounts and system operators require elevated access to critical resources, making them high-value targets for attackers. Identity Federation enables organizations to implement just-in-time (JIT) privileged access, granting temporary permissions based on need and revoking them automatically after the session ends. By federating privileged identities, organizations reduce the risk of credential theft, enforce least privilege access, and ensure that administrative activities are logged and auditable.

Identity Federation enhances Zero Trust in multi-cloud and hybrid environments by providing seamless authentication across cloud service providers and enterprise applications. Organizations often use multiple cloud platforms, each with its own identity management system, leading to fragmented access controls and inconsistent security policies. Federated identity solutions integrate with cloud identity providers such as Microsoft Azure AD, AWS IAM, and Google Cloud Identity, enabling unified authentication across different cloud environments. This ensures that users can securely access cloud workloads while maintaining Zero Trust security controls such as adaptive authentication and conditional access policies.

User behavior analytics (UBA) and threat intelligence further strengthen Identity Federation within Zero Trust architectures. By continuously analyzing authentication patterns, access history, and device activity, identity federation solutions detect anomalies that may indicate compromised credentials or insider threats. If a federated identity exhibits unusual behavior, such as logging in from multiple locations within a short time frame or attempting to access unauthorized systems, the system can trigger automated security responses. These may include requiring additional authentication, revoking access, or alerting security teams for further investigation.

Compliance and regulatory requirements drive the need for strong identity federation in Zero Trust implementations. Regulations such as GDPR, HIPAA, and PCI DSS mandate strict access controls, user authentication, and identity governance policies. Identity Federation helps organizations enforce compliance by providing centralized authentication, role-based access control (RBAC), and detailed audit logs of all authentication events. By integrating Identity Federation with IAM governance frameworks, organizations ensure that security policies are consistently applied across all systems, reducing the risk of compliance violations.

Third-party access and business partner integrations require federated identity solutions to extend Zero Trust security beyond the organization's internal environment. Many enterprises collaborate with vendors, contractors, and suppliers who need temporary access to specific applications. Traditional identity management approaches require organizations to create separate accounts for external users, increasing the risk of security misconfigurations and unmanaged credentials. Identity Federation enables secure authentication for third-party users through identity brokering, allowing external entities to authenticate using their existing credentials while adhering to Zero Trust policies. This approach ensures that third-party access is tightly controlled, monitored, and revoked when no longer needed.

Zero Trust also applies to machine identities, including service accounts, APIs, and automated processes that interact with enterprise systems. Federated identity management extends to non-human identities, ensuring that API calls and service-to-service communications are authenticated based on trusted identity attributes. OAuth 2.0 and JWT-based authentication mechanisms enable secure API authentication, preventing unauthorized access to sensitive data and cloud services. By federating machine identities, organizations reduce the risk of API abuse, enforce least privilege access for automated processes, and enhance Zero Trust security across digital ecosystems.

Automation and artificial intelligence further enhance the role of Identity Federation in Zero Trust by enabling intelligent identity verification and policy enforcement. AI-driven IAM solutions analyze authentication requests in real time, detecting anomalies, assessing risk, and applying dynamic access controls. If an AI system detects that a user's credentials have been exposed in a data breach, it can automatically trigger password resets, enforce MFA, or temporarily suspend access until identity verification is completed. Automated identity federation workflows streamline authentication processes, ensuring that security policies remain adaptive and responsive to evolving threats.

Identity Federation is a crucial component of Zero Trust, enabling seamless and secure authentication across multiple environments while enforcing continuous verification and risk-based access controls. By integrating federated identity solutions with IAM, ZTNA, PAM, UBA, and AI-driven security analytics, organizations create a scalable and adaptive Zero Trust framework that protects users, applications, and data from evolving cyber threats. As enterprises continue to adopt hybrid IT models and cloud-based services, Identity Federation ensures that authentication remains secure, user-friendly, and compliant with modern security standards.

Least Privilege in DevOps and CI/CD Pipelines

The principle of least privilege (PoLP) is a fundamental security concept that restricts users, applications, and systems to the minimum permissions necessary to perform their tasks. In DevOps environments and Continuous Integration/Continuous Deployment (CI/CD) pipelines, enforcing least privilege is crucial to reducing the attack surface, preventing unauthorized access, and minimizing the impact of security breaches. DevOps practices emphasize speed, automation, and collaboration, but without proper access controls, these efficiencies can introduce security risks. Least privilege ensures that developers, automation tools, and deployment processes operate securely without exposing critical systems to excessive permissions or unnecessary access.

CI/CD pipelines automate software development, testing, and deployment processes, integrating multiple tools, scripts, and services across cloud environments and on-premises infrastructure. These pipelines often require access to sensitive repositories, configuration files, databases, and production environments. However, excessive permissions within CI/CD workflows can lead to privilege escalation, insider threats, and unauthorized code modifications. Implementing least privilege access controls in CI/CD pipelines ensures that each component operates with only the necessary permissions, reducing the risk of misconfigurations, credential leaks, and compromised build processes.

IAM plays a central role in enforcing least privilege in DevOps workflows by managing authentication, authorization, and access policies. Traditional IAM models often grant broad administrative permissions to developers and automation tools, increasing security risks. Role-Based Access Control (RBAC) and Attribute-Based Access Control (ABAC) refine access management by assigning permissions based on job roles, project requirements, and contextual factors such as location, device trust, and security posture. By implementing fine-grained access controls, organizations limit user and system privileges, ensuring that only authorized entities can interact with sensitive CI/CD components.

Secrets management is critical to applying least privilege in DevOps environments, as CI/CD pipelines rely on credentials, API keys, and encryption keys to access cloud services, databases, and third-party integrations. Hardcoded credentials in source code or configuration files pose significant security risks, as they can be exposed through code repositories, logs, or accidental leaks. Secure secrets management solutions, such as HashiCorp Vault, AWS Secrets Manager, and Azure Key Vault, enforce strict access controls, encrypt secrets at rest and in transit, and provide just-in-time (JIT) access to credentials only when needed. By integrating secrets management with IAM policies, organizations prevent unauthorized access to critical resources and reduce the likelihood of credential theft.

Just-in-Time (JIT) access provisioning strengthens least privilege enforcement in DevOps environments by granting temporary permissions only when required. Instead of maintaining standing administrative access, JIT access ensures that developers and automation tools receive elevated privileges for specific tasks, such as deploying code, modifying infrastructure, or troubleshooting production issues. Once the task is completed, permissions are revoked automatically, minimizing the attack surface and preventing privilege abuse. JIT access management integrates with IAM solutions and Privileged Access Management (PAM) platforms, ensuring that access is logged, monitored, and controlled in real time.

Zero Trust principles align with least privilege enforcement in CI/CD pipelines by requiring continuous authentication and authorization before granting access to code repositories, build servers, and deployment environments. Traditional security models assume that users and systems within the corporate network are inherently trusted, but Zero Trust mandates that every access request be verified based on identity, risk assessment, and device security posture. By integrating Zero Trust with DevOps workflows, organizations enforce granular access policies, reduce reliance on perimeter-based security, and protect sensitive infrastructure from insider threats and external attacks.

Network segmentation and micro-segmentation further enhance least privilege security in CI/CD environments by restricting lateral movement between development, testing, and production environments. Without segmentation, a compromised DevOps tool or user account could provide attackers with unrestricted access to critical systems. Micro-segmentation enforces access controls at the workload level, ensuring that developers and CI/CD processes can only interact with designated resources. Software-defined networking (SDN) solutions and cloud security controls enable dynamic segmentation, adjusting access policies based on real-time security evaluations and IAM rules.

Monitoring and auditing access activities in CI/CD pipelines provide visibility into privileged actions, enabling organizations to detect anomalies and enforce compliance with least privilege policies. Security Information and Event Management (SIEM) solutions, coupled with User and Entity Behavior Analytics (UEBA), analyze access logs, identify deviations from normal behavior, and trigger alerts for suspicious activities. If a user or automated process attempts to access an unauthorized resource or modify security-sensitive configurations, real-time security controls can block the action, require additional authentication, or escalate the incident to security teams.

Code signing and integrity verification mechanisms further enhance least privilege security in CI/CD pipelines by ensuring that only authorized code is deployed to production. Without proper validation, attackers can inject malicious code into build processes, compromising applications and infrastructure. Digital signatures, cryptographic hashing, and policy-based enforcement ensure that only verified code artifacts pass through deployment stages. By integrating code integrity checks with IAM policies, organizations prevent unauthorized modifications and maintain trust in the software supply chain.

Compliance and regulatory frameworks, such as GDPR, HIPAA, PCI DSS, and SOC 2, require organizations to enforce strict access controls and implement least privilege principles. DevOps and CI/CD environments must adhere to these security standards by restricting administrative access, securing secrets, and continuously monitoring privileged activities. Identity governance and automated access reviews help organizations maintain compliance by periodically evaluating user and system permissions, identifying excessive privileges, and enforcing corrective actions. By integrating compliance controls with least privilege policies, organizations reduce regulatory risks while improving security posture.

Automating least privilege enforcement in DevOps and CI/CD pipelines requires integration with IAM automation tools, policy-driven access controls, and AI-driven threat detection. AI-enhanced IAM solutions analyze access patterns, detect privilege anomalies, and recommend policy adjustments to minimize security risks. Automated remediation workflows revoke excessive permissions, enforce MFA for high-risk actions, and apply dynamic access policies based on security assessments. By leveraging AI and machine learning, organizations improve least privilege security while reducing manual intervention and administrative overhead.

Least privilege is essential for securing DevOps and CI/CD pipelines, preventing unauthorized access, and protecting critical infrastructure from privilege abuse. By implementing IAM best practices, secrets management, JIT access provisioning, Zero Trust security, and continuous monitoring, organizations enforce strong access controls while maintaining agility in software development and deployment. As DevOps practices continue to evolve, integrating least privilege principles ensures that security remains a foundational component of CI/CD workflows, reducing attack surfaces and safeguarding enterprise applications and data.

Zero Trust and API Security

Zero Trust is a security model that eliminates implicit trust, requiring continuous authentication and authorization before granting access to resources. As organizations increasingly rely on Application Programming Interfaces (APIs) to enable digital transformation, secure cloud integrations, and streamline data exchange, API security has become a critical concern. APIs expose functionalities and data to internal systems, third-party applications, and external users, making them prime targets for cyberattacks. Implementing Zero Trust principles in API security ensures that all API interactions are authenticated, authorized, and continuously monitored to prevent unauthorized access, data breaches, and abuse.

Traditional network security models relied on perimeter-based defenses, assuming that internal communications were inherently trusted while external traffic required scrutiny. This approach is ineffective for API security, as APIs are often exposed beyond the corporate network, allowing partners, customers, and third-party developers to access enterprise services. Zero Trust eliminates this implicit trust by enforcing strict access controls, requiring continuous identity verification, and applying real-time risk assessments to all API requests. Every API call must be authenticated, authorized, and inspected before processing, reducing the risk of unauthorized access and data leakage.

Identity and Access Management (IAM) plays a central role in Zero Trust API security, ensuring that only verified identities can access APIs. Traditional API authentication methods relied on static credentials, such as API keys, username-password combinations, and basic authentication. However, these approaches are vulnerable to credential theft, phishing attacks, and unauthorized sharing. Zero Trust mandates strong authentication mechanisms, such as OAuth 2.0, OpenID Connect (OIDC), and Mutual Transport Layer Security (mTLS), to verify API clients before granting access. These protocols enhance security by enabling token-based authentication, reducing reliance on static credentials, and ensuring that API access is granted based on dynamic security policies.

Multi-Factor Authentication (MFA) further strengthens API security by requiring additional verification before granting access to sensitive endpoints. APIs that handle financial transactions, personal data, or administrative functions should enforce MFA for high-risk actions, preventing attackers from exploiting compromised credentials. Adaptive authentication integrates with Zero Trust API security by analyzing contextual factors, such as request origin, device security posture, and historical access patterns, before enforcing authentication challenges. If an API request originates from an untrusted device or an unusual location, the system can require additional verification or block the request entirely.

Least privilege access is a key Zero Trust principle that restricts API permissions to only what is necessary for a given task. Many organizations expose overly permissive API access, allowing clients to retrieve excessive data or perform unauthorized actions. Implementing Role-Based Access Control (RBAC) and Attribute-Based Access Control (ABAC) for APIs ensures that access permissions are granted based on user roles, job functions, and contextual attributes. Fine-grained access control policies prevent privilege escalation, ensuring that API consumers cannot access sensitive resources beyond their designated scope.

API gateways play a crucial role in enforcing Zero Trust security by acting as intermediaries between API clients and backend services. API gateways provide authentication, authorization, rate limiting, logging, and anomaly detection, ensuring that API traffic is inspected before reaching protected resources. By integrating with IAM platforms, API gateways enforce security policies that verify identities, validate tokens, and restrict access based on predefined rules. They also protect against common API attacks, such as injection attacks, cross-site scripting (XSS), and distributed denial-of-service (DDoS) attacks, by filtering malicious traffic and applying security controls at the API level.

Token-based authentication mechanisms, such as JSON Web Tokens (JWT) and OAuth 2.0 access tokens, enhance API security by ensuring that API clients authenticate dynamically rather than relying on hardcoded credentials. OAuth 2.0 enables secure authorization by allowing API consumers to obtain access tokens from an authorization server, reducing the need for direct credential exchange. JWTs provide self-contained, signed tokens that include user claims and permissions, enabling APIs to verify access without repeatedly querying identity providers. Token expiration, rotation, and revocation policies ensure that access remains temporary and controlled, aligning with Zero Trust security principles.

Zero Trust Network Access (ZTNA) extends API security by enforcing granular access policies for API interactions. Unlike traditional VPNs that grant broad network access, ZTNA ensures that API clients can only communicate with specific endpoints based on continuous verification. If an API client exhibits suspicious behavior, such as repeated failed authentication attempts or unusual data access patterns, ZTNA policies can restrict or revoke access in real time. By integrating ZTNA with API security strategies, organizations prevent unauthorized lateral movement and reduce the risk of API abuse.

Continuous monitoring and anomaly detection enhance Zero Trust API security by identifying suspicious API activity in real time. Security Information and Event Management (SIEM) solutions, combined with User and Entity Behavior Analytics (UEBA), analyze API logs, detect abnormal usage patterns, and trigger security alerts for potential threats. If an API suddenly experiences an unusual spike in requests, attempts to access unauthorized resources, or sends large amounts of data to an external server, automated security responses can block malicious requests, throttle API traffic, or notify security teams for investigation.

Data encryption and integrity verification are essential for securing API communications in a Zero Trust framework. All API traffic should be encrypted using TLS 1.2 or higher to protect data in transit from interception and eavesdropping. Additionally, API responses should include integrity verification mechanisms, such as cryptographic signatures or hash-based message authentication codes (HMACs), ensuring that data remains unaltered during transmission. Enforcing encryption at the API level prevents man-in-the-middle attacks, data tampering, and unauthorized access to sensitive information.

Rate limiting and throttling policies further enhance API security by preventing abuse and mitigating DDoS attacks. Many cyberattacks exploit APIs by sending excessive requests to overload backend systems or extract large volumes of data. API gateways enforce rate limits by restricting the number of requests per second for each client, preventing service disruption and unauthorized data scraping. Throttling mechanisms dynamically adjust API access based on security conditions, blocking or delaying suspicious requests to mitigate potential threats. By applying Zero Trust principles to API rate limiting, organizations ensure that API resources remain available and secure.

Compliance and regulatory requirements, such as GDPR, HIPAA, and PCI DSS, mandate strict access controls and data protection measures for API interactions. Zero Trust API security aligns with these compliance frameworks by enforcing strong authentication, encryption, logging, and audit trails. Organizations must implement API governance policies that define security standards, monitor API access logs, and regularly review API permissions to ensure compliance with regulatory mandates. Automated compliance reporting tools provide visibility into API security posture, helping organizations maintain regulatory adherence while reducing security risks.

Zero Trust API security requires a combination of authentication controls, access management, continuous monitoring, and real-time threat detection to protect API ecosystems. By integrating IAM, API gateways, adaptive authentication, and security analytics, organizations enforce strong security policies that prevent unauthorized access, mitigate threats, and ensure compliance. As APIs continue to power digital transformation and cloud adoption, implementing Zero Trust principles in API security remains a critical strategy for protecting enterprise applications, data, and infrastructure from evolving cyber threats.

Identity Threat Detection and Response (ITDR)

Identity Threat Detection and Response (ITDR) is a critical component of modern cybersecurity strategies, focusing on detecting, mitigating, and responding to threats targeting identities, credentials, and access management systems. As cybercriminals increasingly exploit identity-based attack vectors, organizations must adopt ITDR solutions to protect user accounts, privileged credentials, and authentication mechanisms from compromise. ITDR integrates with Identity and Access Management (IAM), Privileged Access Management (PAM), and Security Information and Event Management (SIEM) systems to provide real-time monitoring, anomaly detection, and automated threat response for identity-related attacks.

Identity-based threats have become one of the most significant cybersecurity risks due to the widespread use of stolen credentials, phishing attacks, and social engineering tactics. Attackers often bypass traditional security defenses by compromising legitimate user accounts, allowing them to move laterally within an organization's network without triggering standard intrusion detection mechanisms. ITDR solutions address this challenge by continuously monitoring authentication events, login patterns, and access behaviors to detect unusual activity indicative of credential compromise or privilege escalation attempts.

Credential theft is one of the primary attack vectors ITDR aims to mitigate. Cybercriminals frequently obtain stolen credentials from data breaches, phishing campaigns, and malware infections, using them to access corporate systems and sensitive data. ITDR solutions integrate with dark web monitoring services to detect when employee credentials appear in leaked databases. If a user's credentials are found in a breach, ITDR can trigger an automated response, such as forcing a password reset, revoking session tokens, or requiring multi-factor authentication (MFA) before allowing further access.

Behavioral analytics plays a crucial role in ITDR, leveraging machine learning to establish a baseline of normal user activity and detect deviations that may indicate identity threats. Traditional security approaches rely on static rules and predefined policies, which can be ineffective against sophisticated identity attacks. ITDR solutions analyze user behavior in real time, identifying anomalies such as unusual login locations, excessive authentication failures, or unexpected access requests. If an employee typically logs in from a corporate office but suddenly attempts to access sensitive systems from an untrusted device in a foreign country, ITDR can flag the activity as suspicious and enforce additional security measures.

Privilege escalation is a common technique used by attackers to gain administrative control over an organization's infrastructure. ITDR continuously monitors role changes, access requests, and privilege assignments to detect unauthorized escalation attempts. If a standard user account suddenly gains administrative privileges or attempts to modify security policies, ITDR can generate alerts, restrict access, or require additional authorization from security teams. By preventing unauthorized privilege escalation, ITDR helps mitigate insider threats, compromised accounts, and privilege misuse.

Session hijacking and token theft are growing concerns in identity security, as attackers use stolen session cookies and access tokens to bypass authentication controls. ITDR solutions detect and mitigate session-based threats by monitoring active sessions for anomalies, such as multiple simultaneous logins from different locations, prolonged inactivity followed by unauthorized actions, or the reuse of expired session tokens. If suspicious activity is detected, ITDR can force session termination, invalidate access tokens, and require reauthentication to ensure that only legitimate users retain access.

ITDR enhances Zero Trust security models by continuously validating user identities and access behaviors. Zero Trust assumes that no user or device should be inherently trusted, requiring ongoing authentication and authorization based on real-time risk assessments. ITDR aligns with this approach by enforcing continuous verification, ensuring that users maintain legitimate access privileges throughout their sessions. If an identity-related threat is detected, ITDR solutions can dynamically adjust access permissions, restrict high-risk actions, or enforce step-up authentication to prevent unauthorized access.

Integration with PAM solutions strengthens ITDR's effectiveness in protecting privileged accounts and administrative credentials. PAM enforces strict access controls for privileged users, requiring just-in-time (JIT) access provisioning and session monitoring. ITDR complements PAM by detecting anomalies in privileged account activity, such as unauthorized remote logins, unusual command execution, or attempts to disable security controls. If ITDR detects a high-risk event involving a privileged account, it can automatically revoke access, lock the account, or notify security teams for immediate investigation.

Automated threat response capabilities enhance ITDR's ability to mitigate identity threats in real time. Instead of relying solely on manual security interventions, ITDR integrates with Security Orchestration, Automation, and Response (SOAR) platforms to automate remediation workflows. If an ITDR system detects a compromised account, it can trigger predefined response actions, such as disabling the account, notifying administrators, or initiating an incident response playbook. Automated responses reduce the time required to contain identity threats, minimizing the risk of data breaches and unauthorized access.

ITDR also addresses insider threats by identifying unusual behavior among employees, contractors, and third-party users. Insider threats can be intentional, such as employees exfiltrating sensitive data, or unintentional, such as users falling victim to phishing attacks. ITDR continuously analyzes access patterns, file transfers, and system interactions to detect indicators of insider threats. If an employee suddenly accesses large volumes of sensitive data outside normal working hours or attempts to modify security settings, ITDR can enforce access restrictions, notify security teams, or trigger an immediate security review.

Cloud identity security is a growing concern as organizations adopt multi-cloud environments and federated identity management. ITDR extends identity threat detection to cloud platforms by monitoring cloud IAM configurations, API authentication events, and cloud-based access logs. Misconfigured cloud identity policies can expose sensitive data to unauthorized users, increasing the risk of cloud breaches. ITDR solutions integrate with cloud security posture management (CSPM) tools to detect misconfigurations, enforce least privilege access, and prevent unauthorized API interactions. By applying ITDR principles to cloud identities, organizations enhance security across distributed environments.

Regulatory compliance mandates strong identity protection measures, making ITDR essential for meeting security and privacy requirements. Regulations such as GDPR, HIPAA, and PCI DSS require organizations to monitor access controls, detect unauthorized access attempts, and protect user identities from cyber threats. ITDR supports compliance efforts by generating audit logs, providing real-time threat detection, and automating identity governance processes. By implementing ITDR, organizations demonstrate their commitment to securing identities, reducing the risk of non-compliance penalties, and maintaining regulatory adherence.

AI-driven ITDR solutions enhance identity security by continuously improving threat detection capabilities. Machine learning models analyze vast amounts of identity-related data, identifying emerging attack patterns and refining detection algorithms. AI enhances ITDR by predicting potential identity threats based on historical attack trends, allowing organizations to take proactive security measures before an incident occurs. By leveraging AI for identity threat detection, organizations strengthen their security posture and reduce the impact of identity-based attacks.

Identity Threat Detection and Response is a vital security strategy that protects user identities, detects credential-based threats, and automates response actions to mitigate security risks. By integrating ITDR with IAM, PAM, SIEM, and Zero Trust architectures, organizations establish a robust identity security framework that continuously monitors, analyzes, and defends against identity-related attacks. As cyber threats continue to evolve, ITDR provides the necessary tools and intelligence to safeguard enterprise identities and prevent unauthorized access to critical systems and data.

Zero Trust Access for Remote Workforces

Zero Trust Access is a security framework designed to protect remote workforces by eliminating implicit trust and enforcing continuous authentication and authorization. With the rise of remote and hybrid work environments, traditional security models that relied on network-based perimeter defenses are no longer effective. Employees, contractors, and third-party users connect from various locations, using different devices and networks, making it essential to adopt a security approach that continuously verifies identity, device trust, and security posture before granting access to corporate resources.

Traditional Virtual Private Networks (VPNs) have been the primary method for securing remote access, but they pose significant security risks. VPNs grant broad network access once a user is authenticated, allowing lateral movement within the internal network if an attacker compromises credentials. Zero Trust Network Access (ZTNA) replaces VPNs by enforcing granular access policies based on identity, context, and real-time risk assessments. Unlike VPNs, which assume users within the network perimeter can be trusted, ZTNA ensures that every access request is verified before granting access to specific applications or services, reducing the attack surface.

Identity and Access Management (IAM) plays a crucial role in Zero Trust for remote workforces by ensuring that only verified users and devices can access corporate resources. Multi-Factor Authentication (MFA) is a fundamental security measure that strengthens authentication by requiring multiple forms of verification, such as passwords, biometrics, or one-time passcodes. Adaptive authentication further enhances security by dynamically adjusting authentication requirements based on risk factors, such as login location, device compliance, and access history. If a user attempts to log in from an unrecognized device or an unusual geographic location, the system can prompt for additional verification or block access entirely.

Device trust is a critical component of Zero Trust Access, ensuring that only secure and compliant devices can connect to corporate applications. Organizations implement Endpoint Detection and Response (EDR) and Mobile Device Management (MDM) solutions to enforce security policies on remote endpoints. These solutions assess device posture, checking for software updates, encryption status, and the presence of security controls before granting access. If a remote employee's device lacks the latest security patches or has been flagged as compromised, Zero Trust policies can restrict access until the device meets compliance standards.

Least privilege access is essential for securing remote workforces, ensuring that users have only the permissions necessary to perform their tasks. Many organizations struggle with excessive permissions, where employees retain access to systems they no longer need. Role-Based Access Control (RBAC) and Attribute-Based Access Control (ABAC) enforce fine-grained access policies, restricting access based on job roles, user attributes, and contextual risk factors. Continuous access reviews help organizations identify and revoke unnecessary permissions, reducing the risk of insider threats and privilege escalation attacks.

Secure cloud access is a key challenge in remote work environments, as employees frequently access cloud-based applications, collaboration tools, and SaaS platforms. Zero Trust extends security controls to cloud services by integrating with cloud IAM solutions such as Azure AD, AWS IAM, and Google Cloud Identity. Federated identity management ensures that users can securely access cloud applications without relying on multiple credentials, while Single Sign-On (SSO) enhances security by centralizing authentication. Conditional access policies further strengthen cloud security by evaluating risk signals before granting access, preventing unauthorized access from unmanaged devices or high-risk locations.

Micro-segmentation enhances Zero Trust security for remote workforces by limiting lateral movement within corporate networks. Traditional network segmentation relied on firewall rules and VLANs, which are insufficient for securing remote users accessing applications from various locations. Micro-segmentation enforces identity-aware access policies, ensuring that remote employees can only interact with authorized resources based on their roles and risk profiles. If a user's credentials are compromised, micro-segmentation prevents attackers from moving laterally within the network, containing the impact of security breaches.

Privileged Access Management (PAM) is essential for securing remote administrative users, such as IT support staff, system administrators, and developers. Privileged accounts are high-value targets for cybercriminals, as they grant access to critical infrastructure and sensitive data. PAM solutions enforce Just-in-Time (JIT) access, ensuring that privileged users receive temporary permissions only when needed. Session monitoring and recording provide visibility into privileged activities, enabling organizations to detect suspicious behavior and enforce accountability. By integrating PAM with Zero Trust, organizations reduce the risk of remote privilege abuse and unauthorized administrative actions.

Zero Trust Access ensures that third-party users, such as contractors, vendors, and business partners, are subject to the same security controls as employees. Many organizations grant long-term credentials to external users, increasing security risks if these accounts are not properly managed. Zero Trust enforces strict access controls for third parties by requiring identity verification, just-in-time access provisioning, and continuous monitoring of external user activities. Organizations also implement Zero Trust Network Access (ZTNA) to ensure that third-party users cannot move laterally within the network, restricting them to specific applications and resources based on real-time security assessments.

Continuous monitoring and anomaly detection strengthen Zero Trust security for remote workforces by identifying suspicious activities in real time. Traditional security models relied on periodic audits and static policies, which fail to detect modern threats such as account takeovers, credential stuffing, and remote malware infections. Security Information and Event Management (SIEM) solutions, combined with

User and Entity Behavior Analytics (UEBA), analyze remote access logs, detect anomalies, and trigger automated responses to potential security incidents. If a remote employee's account exhibits unusual behavior, such as accessing corporate systems outside normal working hours or transferring large amounts of data, Zero Trust policies can enforce additional verification steps or terminate the session.

Data protection is a critical aspect of Zero Trust Access for remote workforces, ensuring that sensitive information remains secure regardless of user location. Data Loss Prevention (DLP) solutions monitor data transfers, block unauthorized file sharing, and enforce encryption policies for sensitive documents. Cloud Access Security Brokers (CASBs) provide additional security for cloud-based applications, enforcing policies that prevent data exposure through unmanaged devices or insecure file-sharing services. By integrating DLP and CASB solutions with Zero Trust, organizations ensure that remote employees handle corporate data securely while maintaining compliance with industry regulations.

Zero Trust Access enhances regulatory compliance by enforcing strict access controls, identity verification, and data protection measures. Regulations such as GDPR, HIPAA, and PCI DSS require organizations to secure remote access to sensitive data and maintain audit logs of authentication events. Zero Trust frameworks align with these compliance requirements by implementing strong authentication, continuous monitoring, and automated security responses to unauthorized access attempts. Organizations leverage IAM governance and compliance reporting tools to track remote access activities, ensuring adherence to security policies and regulatory standards.

Automation and artificial intelligence further improve Zero Trust security for remote workforces by enabling proactive threat detection and response. AI-driven IAM solutions analyze authentication patterns, detect anomalies, and apply real-time risk assessments to prevent identity-based attacks. Automated security policies dynamically adjust access permissions based on risk scores, reducing human intervention while improving security efficiency. AI-enhanced behavioral analytics identify deviations from normal user activity, enabling organizations to respond to threats before they escalate. By integrating automation with Zero Trust Access, organizations strengthen security while maintaining a seamless user experience for remote employees.

Zero Trust Access provides a scalable and adaptive security framework for remote workforces, ensuring that users, devices, and applications are continuously verified before accessing corporate resources. By enforcing identity-centric security controls, least privilege access, micro-segmentation, and continuous monitoring, organizations reduce the risk of remote security threats while enabling secure and productive work-from-anywhere capabilities. As hybrid work environments continue to evolve, implementing Zero Trust remains essential for protecting enterprise data, preventing unauthorized access, and maintaining compliance across distributed IT ecosystems.

IAM Compliance and Regulatory Considerations

Identity and Access Management (IAM) plays a critical role in ensuring compliance with regulatory frameworks and industry standards that govern data protection, user authentication, and access control. As organizations handle sensitive information, including personally identifiable information (PII), financial records, and intellectual property, compliance with security regulations becomes a fundamental requirement. Regulatory bodies and industry-specific mandates enforce strict guidelines on identity management, access governance, authentication controls, and auditability to prevent unauthorized access, data breaches, and misuse of privileges.

Regulations such as the General Data Protection Regulation (GDPR), the Health Insurance Portability and Accountability Act (HIPAA), the Payment Card Industry Data Security Standard (PCI DSS), and the Sarbanes-Oxley Act (SOX) impose stringent IAM policies to protect user identities and enforce accountability. Compliance requirements often mandate multi-factor authentication (MFA), least privilege access, continuous monitoring, and detailed audit logging to track user activities across systems. Organizations must align their IAM strategies with these regulations to ensure security while avoiding financial penalties and reputational damage.

Access control is a fundamental requirement in IAM compliance, ensuring that users are granted the minimum level of access necessary for their roles. Role-Based Access Control (RBAC) and Attribute-Based Access Control (ABAC) provide structured methods for managing access permissions based on job functions, contextual attributes, and risk assessments. Regulatory standards such as PCI DSS require organizations to enforce least privilege access, ensuring that only authorized personnel can access sensitive payment data. IAM solutions implement fine-grained access control policies, preventing privilege creep and reducing the risk of unauthorized data exposure.

Multi-Factor Authentication (MFA) is a key security control mandated by many compliance frameworks to prevent unauthorized access due to compromised credentials. Regulations such as GDPR and HIPAA require strong authentication mechanisms to protect sensitive information. IAM solutions enforce MFA policies based on user risk levels, adaptive authentication mechanisms, and behavioral analytics. By requiring additional authentication factors beyond passwords, organizations enhance security and reduce the risk of credential-based attacks, such as phishing and brute-force login attempts.

Identity lifecycle management ensures compliance by governing user provisioning, access modifications, and deprovisioning processes. Regulations such as SOX and GDPR mandate strict user identity governance, ensuring that employee access rights are granted, reviewed, and revoked in a timely manner. IAM automation streamlines onboarding and offboarding workflows, integrating with HR systems to synchronize identity attributes and enforce real-time access changes. Automated access reviews prevent orphaned accounts, reducing the risk of insider threats and unauthorized access to corporate resources.

Privileged Access Management (PAM) plays a crucial role in compliance by securing administrative accounts, system credentials, and high-risk access. Regulatory mandates such as NIST 800-53 and PCI DSS require organizations to implement strict controls over privileged accounts, ensuring that administrative actions are logged, monitored, and restricted based on just-in-time (JIT) access policies. PAM solutions enforce least privilege for system administrators, developers, and security personnel, preventing unauthorized privilege escalation and insider attacks. Session monitoring and privileged activity logging provide forensic audit trails, enabling compliance with industry regulations.

Audit logging and continuous monitoring are essential compliance requirements, ensuring that organizations maintain visibility into authentication events, access requests, and user activities. Regulations such as GDPR and SOX mandate real-time monitoring of IAM-related activities to detect suspicious behavior, security anomalies, and policy violations. Security Information and Event Management (SIEM) solutions integrate with IAM platforms to collect, analyze, and correlate identity-related events. By leveraging machine learning and behavioral analytics, organizations detect potential security threats, enforce compliance policies, and generate audit reports for regulatory assessments.

Data protection and encryption policies align IAM with compliance mandates, securing sensitive information from unauthorized access and exposure. Regulations such as GDPR and HIPAA require organizations to implement encryption for data at rest and in transit, ensuring that authentication credentials, user data, and access logs remain protected. IAM solutions enforce encryption policies through strong cryptographic algorithms, secure authentication tokens, and encrypted storage of identity attributes. By integrating IAM with Data Loss Prevention (DLP) tools, organizations prevent unauthorized data sharing and enforce access restrictions based on security classifications.

Regulatory frameworks emphasize the importance of risk-based access controls, requiring organizations to implement adaptive security measures that respond to changing threat landscapes. IAM compliance strategies incorporate continuous risk assessment models, evaluating user behavior, device trust, and contextual risk factors before granting access. Zero Trust principles align with compliance mandates by enforcing strict authentication requirements, dynamic access controls, and continuous verification of user identities. By integrating IAM with risk-based authentication and threat intelligence platforms, organizations maintain compliance while strengthening identity security.

Third-party access management is a compliance requirement that governs how external vendors, contractors, and business partners access corporate systems. Regulations such as ISO 27001 and PCI DSS require organizations to enforce strict access controls for third parties, ensuring that external users do not have unnecessary permissions or unrestricted access. IAM solutions enforce just-in-time access provisioning for third-party accounts, granting temporary permissions based on business needs. By implementing identity federation and secure authentication gateways, organizations ensure that third-party access aligns with compliance policies while minimizing security risks.

Regulatory compliance mandates periodic access reviews, requiring organizations to evaluate and validate user access rights regularly. IAM solutions automate access certification processes, ensuring that managers and security teams review permissions based on business roles, security policies, and compliance requirements. Regulations such as SOX and HIPAA mandate periodic audits of privileged accounts, ensuring that administrative access remains restricted to authorized personnel. By integrating IAM governance frameworks with compliance monitoring tools, organizations streamline audit processes, enforce policy adherence, and reduce the risk of regulatory violations.

IAM compliance extends to cloud environments, requiring organizations to enforce security policies across hybrid and multi-cloud infrastructures. Cloud IAM solutions, such as AWS IAM, Azure

Active Directory, and Google Cloud Identity, implement compliance controls that align with regulatory frameworks. Cloud Security Posture Management (CSPM) solutions integrate with IAM platforms to detect misconfigurations, excessive permissions, and policy violations. By continuously monitoring cloud IAM policies and enforcing least privilege access, organizations maintain regulatory compliance while securing cloud-based resources.

Artificial intelligence (AI) and automation enhance IAM compliance by enabling intelligent access governance, risk-based authentication, and anomaly detection. AI-driven IAM solutions analyze access patterns, detect policy violations, and recommend corrective actions to ensure compliance with security regulations. Automated remediation workflows enforce security policies, revoking excessive permissions, requiring additional authentication for high-risk users, and generating compliance reports for audit purposes. By leveraging AI for IAM compliance, organizations reduce manual oversight while maintaining strong identity security controls.

IAM compliance and regulatory considerations require organizations to implement strong authentication controls, enforce least privilege access, continuously monitor user activities, and maintain audit trails. By integrating IAM with Zero Trust principles, AI-driven security analytics, and automated compliance tools, organizations achieve regulatory adherence while strengthening identity security. As regulatory requirements continue to evolve, IAM remains a foundational component of security governance, ensuring that access to corporate resources remains secure, compliant, and aligned with industry best practices.

Risk-Based Authentication and Adaptive IAM Policies

Risk-based authentication (RBA) and adaptive Identity and Access Management (IAM) policies are essential components of modern cybersecurity strategies, ensuring that access to corporate resources is granted based on real-time risk assessments rather than static credentials. Traditional authentication models rely on fixed rules, such as username and password combinations, to verify users, but these methods are increasingly vulnerable to credential theft, phishing attacks, and brute-force attempts. Risk-based authentication enhances security by evaluating multiple risk factors before granting access, dynamically adjusting authentication requirements based on user behavior, device posture, location, and historical access patterns.

Adaptive IAM policies take this approach further by continuously monitoring risk levels and modifying access permissions in response to changing security conditions. Unlike static IAM policies that grant or deny access based on predefined roles, adaptive IAM dynamically enforces access controls by analyzing contextual signals and adjusting permissions in real time. This ensures that users receive the least privilege necessary for their current session while reducing friction for legitimate access attempts. By integrating risk-based authentication and adaptive IAM policies, organizations strengthen security, improve user experience, and minimize the risk of unauthorized access.

Risk-based authentication assigns a risk score to each authentication attempt, determining whether access should be granted, denied, or require additional verification. This score is calculated based on various factors, including user behavior, device trust, network security, and threat intelligence. If a login request originates from an unrecognized location, a compromised device, or an IP address associated with malicious activity, the system can enforce additional authentication steps, such as multi-factor authentication (MFA), biometric verification, or security challenge questions. If the risk level is low, access may be granted with minimal friction to improve user experience while maintaining security.

User behavior analytics (UBA) enhances risk-based authentication by detecting anomalies in authentication patterns. Machine learning models analyze historical login data, establishing a baseline for typical user behavior. If a user suddenly attempts to log in from multiple locations within a short timeframe, accesses systems they have never used before, or exhibits an unusually high number of failed login attempts, RBA can flag the activity as suspicious and trigger security actions. These may include requiring step-up authentication, notifying security teams, or temporarily restricting access until further verification is completed.

Device posture assessment plays a crucial role in adaptive IAM policies, ensuring that only secure and compliant devices can access corporate systems. Organizations implement endpoint detection and response (EDR) and mobile device management (MDM) solutions to evaluate device health before granting access. Risk-based authentication considers factors such as operating system version, security patch levels, encryption status, and the presence of malware before determining access privileges. If a user attempts to log in from an outdated or untrusted device, adaptive IAM policies can restrict access, enforce additional security checks, or require device remediation before allowing authentication.

Geolocation and IP reputation analysis further refine risk-based authentication by identifying high-risk access attempts. If a user logs in from a country where they have no previous login history or from an IP address flagged for malicious activity, the system can require additional authentication or block the attempt entirely. Adaptive IAM policies integrate with global threat intelligence feeds to detect suspicious network activity, dynamically adjusting access controls to mitigate risks associated with credential stuffing, bot attacks, and location spoofing.

Context-aware authentication is another critical feature of adaptive IAM policies, dynamically adjusting authentication requirements based on real-time contextual factors. For example, if a user is logging in during normal business hours from a corporate office using a trusted device, authentication requirements may be minimal. However, if the same user attempts to access sensitive data from an unmanaged device over a public Wi-Fi network, the system can enforce stricter authentication policies, such as requiring hardware-based security keys or biometric verification. By tailoring authentication based on risk context, organizations balance security and usability while reducing unnecessary friction for legitimate users.

Risk-based authentication integrates seamlessly with Zero Trust security models, enforcing continuous verification of users and devices. Zero Trust assumes that no user or system should be inherently trusted, requiring ongoing authentication and authorization throughout the session. Adaptive IAM policies align with this approach by dynamically reassessing trust levels, ensuring that access permissions remain appropriate based on evolving risk conditions. If a user's behavior deviates from normal activity, adaptive IAM can revoke access, enforce additional verification steps, or escalate security controls to prevent potential threats.

Privileged Access Management (PAM) benefits significantly from risk-based authentication and adaptive IAM policies, ensuring that administrative and high-risk accounts are subject to stringent access controls. Privileged users, such as system administrators and cloud engineers, require elevated permissions to perform critical tasks, but these accounts are also prime targets for cyberattacks. Risk-based authentication evaluates the risk associated with privileged access requests, enforcing additional security measures such as just-in-time (JIT) access provisioning, session monitoring, and real-time behavior analysis. If an administrator suddenly attempts to modify security configurations from an untrusted device, adaptive IAM can trigger an immediate security review before granting access.

Cloud security and remote access management require risk-based authentication to prevent unauthorized access across distributed environments. As organizations adopt hybrid IT infrastructures, employees and third-party users access applications from multiple devices, networks, and locations. Adaptive IAM policies enforce conditional access controls based on cloud security postures, device compliance, and authentication risk levels. Cloud identity providers, such as Azure AD, AWS IAM, and Google Cloud Identity, integrate with risk-based authentication frameworks to ensure that cloud-based access remains secure and resilient against identity-based threats.

Regulatory compliance frameworks, including GDPR, HIPAA, PCI DSS, and SOX, mandate strict authentication controls to protect sensitive data and prevent unauthorized access. Risk-based authentication helps organizations meet these compliance requirements by enforcing strong authentication policies, logging authentication events, and providing audit trails for security assessments. Adaptive IAM policies automate compliance enforcement, ensuring that users maintain appropriate access privileges while reducing the risk of data breaches and policy violations. By integrating risk-based authentication with compliance monitoring tools, organizations enhance security governance while streamlining audit processes.

Artificial intelligence (AI) and automation further enhance risk-based authentication and adaptive IAM policies by continuously analyzing authentication data, detecting emerging threats, and applying real-time security controls. AI-driven IAM solutions use predictive analytics to identify high-risk authentication attempts, adjusting access policies dynamically based on evolving attack patterns. Automated security responses mitigate identity threats by revoking compromised credentials, enforcing security patches, or triggering incident response actions before security breaches occur. By leveraging AI for risk-based authentication, organizations improve threat detection, reduce false positives, and enhance overall identity security.

Risk-based authentication and adaptive IAM policies provide a dynamic and intelligent approach to identity security, ensuring that access decisions are continuously evaluated based on risk factors, user behavior, and contextual data. By integrating AI-driven security analytics, Zero Trust principles, and automated remediation workflows, organizations enforce least privilege access, prevent identity-based threats, and maintain compliance with regulatory standards. As cyber threats evolve, risk-based authentication remains a critical security control for protecting enterprise identities, reducing unauthorized access risks, and enhancing overall IAM resilience.

Least Privilege in Endpoint Security

Least privilege is a fundamental security principle that ensures users, applications, and processes have only the minimum level of access necessary to perform their tasks. In endpoint security, enforcing least privilege reduces the attack surface, mitigates the risk of malware execution, and prevents unauthorized access to critical systems. Endpoints, including laptops, desktops, mobile devices, and IoT devices, are common entry points for cyber threats. By applying least privilege principles, organizations strengthen endpoint security and minimize the impact of compromised accounts, malware infections, and privilege escalation attacks.

Traditional endpoint security models often grant excessive permissions to users and applications, increasing security risks. Many employees operate with local administrator privileges, allowing them to install software, modify system configurations, and execute scripts that could introduce vulnerabilities. Attackers exploit these elevated privileges to execute malicious code, install persistent backdoors, or disable security controls. Enforcing least privilege removes unnecessary administrator rights, ensuring that users and applications operate with standard permissions unless explicitly required. This prevents attackers from leveraging compromised endpoints to escalate their access within the network.

Privilege escalation is a common attack technique used by cybercriminals to gain higher levels of access on compromised endpoints. Attackers often exploit software vulnerabilities, misconfigured access controls, or stolen credentials to elevate their privileges from standard user accounts to administrator or system-level access. By enforcing least privilege, organizations limit the ability of malware and attackers to execute privileged commands, reducing the likelihood of system compromise. Endpoint protection platforms (EPP) and Endpoint Detection and Response (EDR) solutions detect and block privilege escalation attempts, enhancing security by continuously monitoring endpoint activities.

Application control and allowlisting further strengthen least privilege enforcement by restricting the execution of unauthorized applications. Traditional endpoint security solutions rely on antivirus signatures to detect malware, but advanced threats often bypass these defenses through fileless attacks and zero-day exploits. Allowlisting policies ensure that only approved applications can run on endpoints, preventing unauthorized software installations and malicious script execution. By integrating application control with least privilege policies, organizations reduce the risk of unauthorized code execution, ransomware infections, and supply chain attacks.

Just-in-Time (JIT) privilege elevation provides a flexible approach to least privilege enforcement, granting temporary administrative rights only when necessary. Instead of permanently assigning administrator privileges to users or applications, JIT access ensures that elevated permissions are granted dynamically for specific tasks and revoked immediately after use. Privileged Access Management (PAM) solutions implement JIT access on endpoints, allowing IT teams to manage administrative privileges securely without increasing security risks. By limiting the duration of elevated access, JIT privilege elevation prevents attackers from exploiting long-term administrative credentials.

Zero Trust security models align with least privilege in endpoint security by continuously verifying identity, device compliance, and access requests. Unlike traditional security approaches that assume trusted internal users, Zero Trust requires endpoints to authenticate and validate security posture before accessing corporate resources. Least privilege enforcement ensures that endpoints cannot access unauthorized systems or sensitive data unless explicitly permitted. By integrating Zero Trust with endpoint security policies, organizations enforce continuous verification, reducing the risk of lateral movement and unauthorized data access.

Remote work and bring-your-own-device (BYOD) policies introduce additional challenges for enforcing least privilege on endpoints. Employees often use personal devices to access corporate applications, increasing security risks if those devices are compromised. Mobile Device Management (MDM) and Endpoint Detection and Response (EDR) solutions enforce least privilege on remote endpoints by controlling device permissions, restricting access to corporate networks, and ensuring compliance with security policies. If an unmanaged or non-compliant device attempts to access enterprise systems, least privilege policies can block access or require additional authentication before granting permissions.

Privileged Access Workstations (PAWs) provide a secure endpoint environment for users with administrative responsibilities, reducing the risk of privileged credential compromise. Instead of allowing privileged users to perform administrative tasks from standard workstations, PAWs are configured with strict security policies, network isolation, and least privilege access controls. These workstations are dedicated to high-risk activities, such as system administration and critical infrastructure management, ensuring that privileged credentials are not exposed to internet-facing threats or phishing attacks. By enforcing least privilege on PAWs, organizations mitigate the risk of privilege abuse and insider threats.

Endpoint security solutions integrate with IAM frameworks to enforce least privilege policies based on user roles, security context, and behavioral analytics. Role-Based Access Control (RBAC) and Attribute-Based Access Control (ABAC) dynamically adjust endpoint permissions based on job functions, device security posture, and contextual risk factors. If a user attempts to access high-risk applications from an untrusted device, least privilege policies can restrict permissions, enforce multi-factor authentication (MFA), or require additional verification before allowing access. By integrating IAM with endpoint security, organizations ensure that least privilege enforcement remains adaptive and risk-based.

Security monitoring and anomaly detection enhance least privilege enforcement by identifying suspicious activities on endpoints. User and Entity Behavior Analytics (UEBA) solutions analyze endpoint interactions, detecting deviations from normal behavior that may indicate credential theft, insider threats, or malware activity. If an endpoint suddenly exhibits unusual privilege escalation attempts, unauthorized software installations, or unexpected data transfers, security teams can respond by revoking access, isolating the endpoint, or triggering automated remediation actions. Continuous monitoring ensures that least privilege policies remain effective in preventing endpoint-based attacks.

Regulatory compliance frameworks, including GDPR, HIPAA, PCI DSS, and NIST 800-53, require organizations to enforce least privilege access controls on endpoints. Compliance mandates emphasize the need for strong authentication, restricted administrator privileges, and audit logging of privileged activities. Organizations implement least privilege policies to meet these regulatory requirements, ensuring that endpoints operate within compliance boundaries. Security audits and access reviews validate endpoint permissions, identifying and correcting excessive privileges before they become security risks. By integrating compliance monitoring with least privilege enforcement, organizations reduce regulatory exposure while strengthening endpoint security.

AI-driven security automation further enhances least privilege enforcement on endpoints by detecting and responding to emerging threats in real time. Machine learning models analyze endpoint behavior, identifying privilege anomalies, unauthorized software execution, and suspicious access patterns. Automated remediation workflows dynamically adjust endpoint permissions, revoke excessive privileges, and enforce security policies based on real-time threat intelligence. By leveraging AI for endpoint security, organizations improve least privilege enforcement while reducing manual intervention and administrative overhead.

Implementing least privilege in endpoint security reduces the risk of malware infections, privilege escalation, and unauthorized access to critical systems. By enforcing role-based access controls, just-in-time privilege elevation, application allowlisting, and continuous security monitoring, organizations ensure that endpoints operate securely while minimizing attack vectors. As cyber threats continue to evolve, integrating least privilege principles with IAM, Zero Trust, and AI-driven security automation remains essential for protecting enterprise endpoints and maintaining a strong security posture.

Zero Trust for Internet of Things (IoT) Devices

Zero Trust is a security model that eliminates implicit trust and enforces continuous authentication and authorization for every device, user, and application before granting access. As the adoption of Internet of Things (IoT) devices grows across industries, securing these devices becomes a critical challenge. IoT devices are often deployed in uncontrolled environments, lack traditional security controls, and operate with minimal user oversight. Implementing Zero Trust for IoT devices ensures that each device is verified, its behavior is continuously monitored, and access to network resources is restricted based on real-time risk assessments.

IoT devices introduce unique security risks due to their diverse architectures, operating systems, and communication protocols. Many IoT devices have default credentials, weak encryption, and limited security update mechanisms, making them attractive targets for cybercriminals. Traditional network security models assume that devices within the corporate perimeter can be trusted, but Zero Trust eliminates this assumption. Every IoT device must authenticate before accessing resources, and continuous monitoring ensures that anomalous behavior is detected and mitigated in real time.

Device identity and authentication are foundational principles of Zero Trust for IoT security. Unlike traditional IT endpoints, IoT devices often lack user-managed authentication mechanisms, requiring alternative identity verification methods. Organizations implement device certificates, cryptographic authentication, and hardware-based security modules to establish unique identities for IoT devices. Mutual Transport Layer Security (mTLS) ensures that devices authenticate both to the network and to cloud services before transmitting data. By enforcing strong identity verification, Zero Trust prevents unauthorized devices from connecting to enterprise networks and critical infrastructure.

Least privilege access is a key Zero Trust principle that restricts IoT devices to the minimum permissions necessary for operation. Many IoT devices are configured with broad network access, allowing attackers to exploit vulnerabilities and move laterally across the network. Implementing Role-Based Access Control (RBAC) and Attribute-Based Access Control (ABAC) ensures that IoT devices can only interact with authorized systems and services. If an IoT device is designed to collect temperature data, it should not have access to sensitive enterprise databases or administrative network functions. Enforcing least privilege limits the potential damage caused by compromised devices.

Micro-segmentation enhances Zero Trust security by isolating IoT devices from critical systems. Unlike traditional network segmentation, which relies on firewalls and VLANs, micro-segmentation applies identity-aware access controls that dynamically restrict device communication based on security policies. If an IoT security camera is compromised, micro-segmentation prevents it from accessing enterprise applications, limiting the attack surface. Software-defined networking (SDN) and identity-based network policies ensure that IoT devices are segmented based on risk levels, preventing unauthorized data flows and reducing exposure to cyber threats.

Zero Trust Network Access (ZTNA) replaces legacy VPN-based access models for IoT devices, ensuring that devices must authenticate before accessing enterprise resources. VPNs often grant broad network access once a device is authenticated, creating security risks if an IoT device is compromised. ZTNA enforces per-session authentication and continuously evaluates device trust levels. If an IoT sensor in a manufacturing facility exhibits unusual traffic patterns, Zero Trust policies can revoke access, enforce reauthentication, or quarantine the device for further analysis.

Continuous monitoring and anomaly detection strengthen Zero Trust for IoT devices by identifying suspicious behavior in real time. IoT devices generate large volumes of telemetry data, making manual security monitoring impractical. Security Information and Event Management (SIEM) platforms, combined with User and Entity Behavior Analytics (UEBA), analyze IoT traffic, detect deviations from normal activity, and trigger automated security responses. If an industrial IoT device starts communicating with unauthorized IP addresses, security policies can block the connection and alert administrators. By leveraging AI-driven analytics, organizations can detect IoT threats before they escalate into security incidents.

Firmware and software integrity verification ensure that IoT devices operate securely within Zero Trust environments. Many IoT attacks exploit vulnerabilities in outdated firmware, allowing attackers to deploy malicious code or create backdoors. Zero Trust enforces strict update policies, requiring cryptographic signatures and integrity checks before applying firmware updates. Secure boot mechanisms prevent unauthorized code execution, ensuring that only trusted firmware versions run on IoT devices. By integrating Zero Trust with endpoint security frameworks, organizations maintain the integrity of IoT deployments and prevent unauthorized modifications.

IoT security posture management (IoT-SPM) aligns with Zero Trust principles by continuously assessing device configurations, vulnerabilities, and compliance risks. Organizations implement automated IoT risk assessments to detect misconfigured devices, enforce security baselines, and remediate potential threats. If an IoT medical device in a hospital network is running outdated software, Zero Trust policies can flag it for remediation before allowing network access. IoT-SPM solutions integrate with identity management platforms to enforce compliance with security standards, ensuring that only trusted devices operate within enterprise environments.

Data encryption and secure communication channels are critical components of Zero Trust for IoT devices. Many IoT devices transmit sensitive data, including personal information, industrial telemetry, and business intelligence, making them prime targets for data interception. Zero Trust enforces encryption for data in transit and at rest, ensuring that unauthorized entities cannot access sensitive information. Secure communication protocols, such as TLS 1.3, MQTT with encryption, and end-to-end encryption (E2EE), protect data integrity and confidentiality. By enforcing encrypted communication channels, Zero Trust mitigates the risk of data leaks and man-in-the-middle attacks.

Regulatory compliance frameworks, including GDPR, HIPAA, and NIST 800-183, require strong security controls for IoT devices. Zero Trust aligns with these compliance mandates by enforcing strict identity verification, least privilege access, continuous monitoring, and data protection policies. Organizations implement Zero Trust policies to ensure that IoT devices meet regulatory security requirements, reducing the risk of compliance violations and legal penalties. Audit logging and security reporting provide visibility into IoT security events, enabling organizations to demonstrate compliance during regulatory assessments.

Supply chain security is an essential aspect of Zero Trust for IoT devices, preventing unauthorized components and firmware from entering enterprise environments. Many IoT devices are manufactured by third-party vendors, increasing the risk of supply chain attacks. Zero Trust enforces security validation at every stage of the IoT lifecycle, requiring device manufacturers to implement secure development practices, firmware integrity verification, and cryptographic attestation. If an IoT device is sourced from an unverified supplier, security policies can block its deployment until it passes compliance checks. By securing the IoT supply chain, organizations prevent the introduction of compromised devices into their networks.

Zero Trust automation and artificial intelligence improve IoT security by dynamically adjusting access policies, detecting threats, and enforcing compliance. AI-driven IoT security solutions analyze device behavior, identify anomalies, and apply automated remediation actions to contain potential threats. If an IoT-connected surveillance camera exhibits abnormal network traffic, AI-driven security controls can isolate the device, enforce security patches, or notify administrators for further investigation. By leveraging AI and automation, organizations enhance Zero Trust for IoT devices, ensuring that security remains adaptive and responsive to emerging threats.

Zero Trust provides a scalable and effective security framework for IoT devices, ensuring that every device is authenticated, continuously monitored, and restricted based on real-time risk assessments. By implementing strong identity verification, least privilege access, micro-segmentation, and continuous monitoring, organizations reduce the attack surface and prevent unauthorized access to IoT infrastructure. As IoT adoption continues to expand, Zero Trust remains essential for securing connected devices, protecting sensitive data, and maintaining compliance with evolving cybersecurity regulations.

Data Security and Identity-Centric Zero Trust

Data security is a critical component of Zero Trust, ensuring that access to sensitive information is strictly controlled, continuously verified, and dynamically adjusted based on identity and risk factors. Traditional security models relied on network perimeters to protect data, assuming that users and devices inside the organization's network were inherently trusted. This approach is no longer effective, as cyber threats increasingly exploit stolen credentials, insider risks, and misconfigured cloud environments to gain unauthorized access to sensitive data. Identity-centric Zero Trust shifts security from a network-based model to one that prioritizes authentication, authorization, and continuous monitoring of user and entity behaviors to protect data at every access point.

Zero Trust enforces least privilege access to data, ensuring that users, applications, and systems only have access to the minimum amount of information required for their tasks. Many organizations suffer from overprivileged access, where employees retain unnecessary permissions to sensitive data due to poor access management practices. Role-Based Access Control (RBAC) and Attribute-Based Access Control (ABAC) enforce fine-grained permissions, restricting data access based on job roles, contextual factors, and real-time security assessments. If an employee requires access to financial records, identity-centric Zero Trust ensures that they can only retrieve data relevant to their job function, preventing unnecessary exposure to confidential information.

Multi-Factor Authentication (MFA) strengthens data security by requiring additional verification before granting access to sensitive resources. Passwords alone are insufficient for protecting data, as they can be easily compromised through phishing attacks, credential stuffing, and brute-force attempts. Zero Trust enforces MFA for high-risk data access scenarios, such as logging in from untrusted locations, accessing classified files, or performing privileged operations. Adaptive authentication further enhances security by dynamically adjusting authentication requirements based on real-time risk levels. If a user attempts to download a large volume of data from a remote device, the system may require biometric authentication or a time-sensitive one-time passcode to verify legitimacy.

Data classification and encryption are essential components of identity-centric Zero Trust, ensuring that sensitive information remains protected regardless of its location. Organizations categorize data based on sensitivity levels, applying strict access controls and encryption policies to confidential records, intellectual property, and personally identifiable information (PII). Zero Trust requires encryption for data at rest, in transit, and in use, preventing unauthorized access even if an attacker gains access to the storage system. Cloud environments integrate Zero Trust encryption policies with data access controls, ensuring that only authorized users with verified identities can decrypt and access sensitive files.

Zero Trust Network Access (ZTNA) replaces traditional VPN-based security models, ensuring that data access is granted based on continuous verification rather than broad network permissions. VPNs often provide excessive access to network resources, allowing attackers to move laterally once inside the perimeter. ZTNA restricts access to specific applications and data repositories based on user identity, device security posture, and contextual risk factors. If an attacker compromises a user's credentials, ZTNA prevents unrestricted access by enforcing continuous authentication and session monitoring to detect anomalous activity.

Cloud security posture management (CSPM) aligns with identity-centric Zero Trust by continuously assessing cloud data security configurations. Many organizations store sensitive data in multi-cloud environments, increasing the risk of misconfigurations and unauthorized access. Zero Trust integrates CSPM solutions to detect excessive permissions, enforce encryption policies, and identify publicly exposed cloud storage containers. Automated remediation actions ensure that security policies are consistently applied, preventing data leaks and unauthorized modifications to cloud-based records.

Data Loss Prevention (DLP) solutions enforce Zero Trust policies by monitoring and controlling the movement of sensitive information across corporate networks, endpoints, and cloud applications. Organizations implement DLP rules to prevent unauthorized sharing of confidential data via email, removable media, or cloud storage services. If an employee attempts to transfer sensitive files outside approved communication channels, Zero Trust policies can block the action, notify security teams, or enforce encryption before transmission. By integrating DLP with identity-based access controls, organizations ensure that data security policies are consistently enforced across all endpoints and access points.

User and Entity Behavior Analytics (UEBA) enhance data security by detecting anomalies in user activities and access patterns. Zero Trust continuously monitors how users interact with data, identifying deviations from normal behavior that may indicate insider threats, compromised credentials, or data exfiltration attempts. If an employee who typically accesses customer records suddenly attempts to download thousands of files outside normal working hours, UEBA can trigger security alerts, enforce additional authentication requirements, or block the action entirely. By leveraging machine learning and behavioral analytics, Zero Trust minimizes the risk of unauthorized data access while reducing false positives.

Privileged Access Management (PAM) further strengthens identity-centric Zero Trust by securing administrative access to critical data repositories and high-risk systems. Privileged accounts often have extensive access to databases, cloud storage, and file servers, making them prime targets for cyberattacks. Zero Trust enforces just-in-time (JIT) privileged access, granting temporary administrative permissions only when necessary. Session monitoring and activity logging ensure that privileged data interactions are auditable and compliant with security policies. If an administrator attempts to modify access controls for a sensitive database without proper authorization, Zero Trust policies can revoke access and trigger a security investigation.

Regulatory compliance frameworks, including GDPR, HIPAA, PCI DSS, and SOX, mandate strict data protection measures to prevent unauthorized access and breaches. Identity-centric Zero Trust helps organizations meet compliance requirements by enforcing role-based access policies, encryption standards, and continuous monitoring of data access. Security teams use IAM governance tools to generate audit logs, review access controls, and ensure that data protection policies align with regulatory mandates. Automated compliance reporting simplifies security assessments, reducing the risk of non-compliance penalties while improving overall data governance.

Artificial intelligence (AI) and automation enhance data security within a Zero Trust framework by continuously adapting access policies based on evolving threats. AI-driven identity analytics detect emerging attack patterns, automatically adjusting access permissions, revoking compromised credentials, or enforcing step-up authentication for high-risk data access attempts. Automated threat detection reduces the time required to identify and mitigate security incidents, ensuring that data remains protected against sophisticated cyber threats. By leveraging AI-driven automation, organizations strengthen data security while reducing administrative overhead and improving response times.

Zero Trust enforces a data-centric security model, ensuring that sensitive information is continuously protected, access is dynamically controlled, and users are authenticated based on real-time risk assessments. By integrating encryption, adaptive authentication, DLP, UEBA, and AI-driven analytics, organizations reduce the risk of unauthorized data access, insider threats, and credential-based attacks. As cyber threats evolve, identity-centric Zero Trust remains essential for securing enterprise data, maintaining regulatory compliance, and preventing unauthorized access across distributed IT environments.

Zero Trust Challenges and Common Pitfalls

Zero Trust is a transformative security framework that enhances protection by eliminating implicit trust and continuously verifying users, devices, and applications before granting access. While the model significantly improves security, its implementation presents several challenges and common pitfalls that organizations must address to ensure successful adoption. Zero Trust requires a fundamental shift from traditional perimeter-based security models, demanding changes in technology, policies, and organizational mindset. Without careful planning and execution, organizations may face operational inefficiencies, security gaps, and resistance to change.

One of the primary challenges in Zero Trust implementation is the complexity of transitioning from legacy security architectures. Many organizations rely on traditional network perimeter defenses, such as firewalls and VPNs, which assume that internal users and devices can be trusted once authenticated. Shifting to a Zero Trust model requires restructuring access controls, segmenting networks, and enforcing continuous authentication. This transition can be resource-intensive, requiring investments in new technologies, identity management systems, and security automation. Without a clear migration strategy, organizations may struggle to integrate Zero Trust principles into their existing IT infrastructure.

Identity and Access Management (IAM) plays a crucial role in Zero Trust, but ineffective IAM implementations can create security vulnerabilities. Many organizations fail to enforce strict identity verification policies, leading to weak authentication mechanisms and overprivileged accounts. Poorly managed IAM systems may result in excessive access permissions, privilege creep, and orphaned accounts, increasing the risk of insider threats and unauthorized access. Implementing Zero Trust requires robust IAM policies, including Role-Based Access Control (RBAC), Attribute-Based Access Control (ABAC), and continuous access reviews to ensure that users and applications have only the permissions necessary for their tasks.

A common pitfall in Zero Trust implementation is inadequate endpoint security. Zero Trust assumes that every endpoint is a potential threat, requiring continuous monitoring and security enforcement. However, many organizations fail to implement strong endpoint security measures, leaving gaps in device trust verification. Unpatched operating systems, weak endpoint security configurations, and the use of personal or unmanaged devices can introduce security risks. Organizations must integrate Endpoint Detection and Response (EDR) solutions, enforce device compliance policies, and implement Mobile Device Management (MDM) to ensure that only secure endpoints can access corporate resources.

Network segmentation and micro-segmentation are critical components of Zero Trust, but improper implementation can lead to operational disruptions. Many organizations struggle with segmenting their networks effectively, either creating overly restrictive access policies that hinder productivity or failing to enforce adequate segmentation, allowing unauthorized lateral movement. Without proper planning, micro-segmentation efforts may lead to excessive administrative overhead, requiring frequent policy adjustments and manual intervention. Organizations must use automated policy enforcement, identity-aware firewalls, and software-defined networking (SDN) to manage segmentation dynamically without disrupting business operations.

Zero Trust Network Access (ZTNA) replaces traditional VPN-based remote access models, but improper deployment can lead to security gaps. Many organizations implement ZTNA solutions without fully integrating them with IAM, resulting in inconsistent access policies and authentication workflows. Inadequate visibility into ZTNA access logs and session activities can prevent security teams from detecting anomalous behavior and potential security threats. To mitigate these risks, organizations must ensure that ZTNA solutions integrate seamlessly with IAM, SIEM, and User and Entity Behavior Analytics (UEBA) tools for continuous monitoring and threat detection.

Another significant challenge in Zero Trust adoption is user resistance and organizational pushback. Employees and IT teams accustomed to traditional security models may perceive Zero Trust as an obstacle to productivity due to increased authentication steps and access restrictions. If not implemented with user experience in mind, Zero Trust can lead to frustration and workarounds that weaken security, such as sharing credentials or using personal devices to bypass security controls. Organizations must prioritize user training, communicate the benefits of Zero Trust, and implement frictionless authentication methods, such as passwordless authentication and adaptive MFA, to balance security with usability.

Misconfigurations in Zero Trust policies can lead to security vulnerabilities and operational failures. Many organizations rely on manual configuration processes, increasing the likelihood of errors in access policies, firewall rules, and identity verification settings. Improperly configured access controls may grant excessive permissions to users or applications, defeating the purpose of least privilege access. Automated security policy management, AI-driven anomaly detection, and continuous security audits help prevent misconfigurations and ensure that Zero Trust policies remain effective and up to date.

Data security remains a challenge in Zero Trust adoption, as many organizations focus primarily on identity and network controls while neglecting data protection measures. Zero Trust requires a data-centric approach, ensuring that sensitive information is encrypted, classified, and restricted based on access policies. Many organizations fail to implement proper Data Loss Prevention (DLP) strategies, resulting in unauthorized data transfers, misconfigured cloud storage permissions, and exposure of confidential information. Organizations must integrate Zero Trust principles with DLP, Cloud Access Security Brokers (CASB), and encryption frameworks to ensure comprehensive data security.

Zero Trust requires continuous monitoring and threat detection, but many organizations lack the necessary visibility into user activities, access patterns, and security events. Traditional security monitoring tools may not provide real-time insights into Zero Trust environments, leaving blind spots in threat detection. Without integrated security analytics, organizations may struggle to detect identity-based threats, compromised accounts, or privilege escalation attempts. Security Information and Event Management (SIEM), UEBA, and AI-driven security automation provide the necessary visibility to detect and respond to threats effectively.

Compliance and regulatory challenges also complicate Zero Trust implementation. Many organizations operate in regulated industries that require strict access controls, audit logging, and data protection measures. While Zero Trust aligns with compliance frameworks such as GDPR, HIPAA, PCI DSS, and NIST, implementing Zero Trust without proper compliance mapping can lead to regulatory gaps. Organizations must ensure that Zero Trust policies align with legal requirements, automate compliance reporting, and conduct regular security assessments to maintain regulatory adherence.

Zero Trust implementation requires careful planning, integration, and continuous adaptation to avoid security gaps and operational disruptions. Organizations must address challenges related to IAM, endpoint security, network segmentation, data protection, and compliance to ensure the successful adoption of Zero Trust principles. By leveraging automation, AI-driven security analytics, and user-friendly authentication methods, organizations can overcome common pitfalls and build a resilient security framework that protects against evolving cyber threats.

Implementing Zero Trust in Government and Healthcare

Zero Trust is a security model designed to eliminate implicit trust and enforce continuous authentication, authorization, and least privilege access to protect critical systems and sensitive data. In government and healthcare sectors, where data confidentiality, integrity, and availability are paramount, implementing Zero Trust is essential to mitigating cyber threats, preventing unauthorized access, and ensuring compliance with strict regulatory frameworks. Traditional perimeter-based security models are no longer sufficient to protect these highly targeted industries from ransomware, insider threats, and nation-state cyberattacks. Zero Trust provides a modern approach to securing digital assets while enabling secure collaboration across agencies, healthcare providers, and third-party entities.

Government organizations handle highly sensitive information, including classified data, citizen records, and critical infrastructure controls. The increasing adoption of cloud services, remote work, and inter-agency collaboration presents new security challenges, requiring a shift from legacy security models to Zero Trust architectures. Government agencies must verify every user, device, and application before granting access to resources, ensuring that security policies remain dynamic and risk-based. Implementing Identity and Access Management (IAM) frameworks with strong authentication mechanisms, such as multi-factor authentication (MFA) and biometric verification, is a foundational step in Zero Trust for government entities.

Healthcare organizations store and process vast amounts of personally identifiable information (PII) and protected health information (PHI), making them prime targets for cyberattacks. Electronic Health Records (EHRs), medical devices, and cloud-based healthcare platforms require stringent security controls to prevent data breaches and ensure compliance with regulations such as the Health Insurance Portability and Accountability Act (HIPAA) and the General Data Protection Regulation (GDPR). Zero Trust ensures that only authorized medical personnel, administrators, and trusted third parties can access sensitive patient data, reducing the risk of unauthorized exposure or data theft.

Least privilege access is a core principle of Zero Trust in government and healthcare, ensuring that users, applications, and devices have only the minimum permissions necessary to perform their functions. Role-Based Access Control (RBAC) and Attribute-Based Access Control (ABAC) enforce fine-grained access policies, preventing employees from accessing data or systems that are not relevant to their roles. In government environments, Zero Trust policies ensure that military personnel, intelligence officers, and civilian employees only access information based on security clearance levels and contextual risk assessments. In healthcare, Zero Trust limits access to patient records, ensuring that doctors, nurses, and administrative staff can only retrieve medical data necessary for treatment and operational processes.

Network segmentation and micro-segmentation enhance Zero Trust security by preventing lateral movement of threats within government and healthcare networks. Traditional flat network architectures allow attackers to move freely between systems once they gain initial access, increasing the risk of data breaches and infrastructure sabotage. Micro-segmentation applies identity-aware access controls to restrict communication between applications, medical devices, and administrative systems. In government networks, this prevents unauthorized users from accessing classified databases or mission-critical systems. In healthcare environments, micro-segmentation isolates connected medical devices, ensuring that cyberattacks do not spread from one compromised system to another.

Zero Trust Network Access (ZTNA) replaces traditional VPN-based remote access solutions, ensuring that government and healthcare employees, contractors, and vendors can securely connect to applications and data without exposing entire networks. VPNs often provide broad network access, increasing security risks if credentials are compromised. ZTNA enforces per-session authentication, continuous monitoring, and contextual risk evaluations before granting access. Government agencies use ZTNA to secure remote work environments while maintaining strict access controls. Healthcare organizations implement ZTNA to provide secure telemedicine services and enable third-party vendors to access healthcare systems without compromising security.

Endpoint security plays a critical role in Zero Trust for government and healthcare organizations, ensuring that only trusted and compliant devices can access sensitive data and systems. Many cyberattacks exploit vulnerabilities in unpatched endpoints, including workstations, mobile devices, and Internet of Medical Things (IoMT) devices. Zero Trust requires endpoint detection and response (EDR) solutions, mobile device management (MDM), and continuous compliance checks to verify device security posture before allowing access. Government agencies enforce Zero Trust endpoint security to protect classified data and national infrastructure. Healthcare providers apply Zero Trust to medical devices, ensuring that IoMT endpoints remain secure against ransomware attacks and unauthorized modifications.

Privileged Access Management (PAM) strengthens Zero Trust implementation by securing administrative and high-risk user accounts. Privileged users, such as IT administrators, system operators, and healthcare executives, have access to critical government systems and medical databases. Cybercriminals often target privileged accounts to escalate their access and execute high-impact attacks. Zero Trust enforces just-in-time (JIT) privileged access, ensuring that administrative permissions are granted only when necessary and revoked immediately after the session ends. Government agencies implement PAM to prevent insider threats and unauthorized administrative actions. Healthcare organizations use PAM to secure access to EHR systems, financial records, and cloud-based patient data storage.

Data encryption and secure communication channels are essential Zero Trust components for protecting sensitive government and healthcare information. Data in transit and at rest must be encrypted using advanced cryptographic protocols to prevent unauthorized access and interception. Government agencies apply encryption to classified documents, secure email communications, and cloud-based storage environments. Healthcare organizations enforce encryption policies to protect patient records, medical imaging data, and financial transactions. Secure APIs and encrypted data exchanges ensure that digital health platforms, insurance providers, and government healthcare programs maintain Zero Trust principles while enabling secure interoperability.

Regulatory compliance frameworks require government and healthcare organizations to implement strong access controls, continuous monitoring, and data protection measures. Zero Trust aligns with these compliance mandates by enforcing strict authentication, audit logging, and risk-based access policies. Government agencies must comply with the Federal Information Security Management Act (FISMA), the National Institute of Standards and Technology (NIST) guidelines, and country-specific cybersecurity regulations. Healthcare providers adhere to HIPAA, GDPR, and the Cybersecurity Maturity Model Certification (CMMC) to protect patient and insurance data. Zero Trust solutions provide automated compliance reporting, continuous security assessments, and risk-based policy enforcement to ensure regulatory adherence.

Artificial intelligence (AI) and automation enhance Zero Trust implementation in government and healthcare by analyzing access patterns, detecting security anomalies, and enforcing real-time security controls. AI-driven User and Entity Behavior Analytics (UEBA) detect unusual user activities, such as unauthorized access attempts, excessive data downloads, or privilege escalation attempts. Automated security workflows respond to threats by revoking access, triggering security alerts, and isolating compromised accounts. Government agencies use AI-driven Zero Trust security to protect critical infrastructure, intelligence operations, and law enforcement databases. Healthcare providers leverage AI-powered Zero Trust solutions to detect medical fraud, prevent data breaches, and enforce security policies across cloud-based health services.

Government and healthcare organizations face increasing cyber threats, making Zero Trust a necessary security model to protect sensitive data, prevent unauthorized access, and maintain regulatory compliance. By enforcing identity verification, least privilege access, continuous monitoring, and adaptive security controls, Zero Trust strengthens cybersecurity resilience in these highly regulated industries. As digital transformation accelerates, government agencies and healthcare providers must implement Zero Trust frameworks to secure critical operations, protect citizen and patient data, and mitigate evolving cybersecurity risks.

The Future of Zero Trust and IAM Innovations

Zero Trust and Identity and Access Management (IAM) are evolving rapidly as organizations face increasingly sophisticated cyber threats, regulatory requirements, and the challenges of securing distributed IT environments. The future of Zero Trust will be driven by advancements in artificial intelligence (AI), automation, decentralized identity models, and continuous authentication mechanisms. As traditional perimeter-based security models become obsolete, Zero Trust will continue to integrate deeper into IAM strategies, enabling adaptive security policies that dynamically adjust based on user behavior, contextual risk assessments, and real-time threat intelligence.

AI and machine learning will play a critical role in advancing Zero Trust and IAM by enabling intelligent identity verification, anomaly detection, and automated access decision-making. Traditional IAM solutions rely on static access policies and predefined rules, which can be ineffective against emerging threats. AI-driven IAM continuously analyzes authentication patterns, login behaviors, and access requests, identifying potential security risks before they escalate. By leveraging machine learning algorithms, organizations can detect suspicious activities, such as unusual login attempts, privilege escalation, or compromised credentials, and enforce real-time security responses. AI-powered risk-based authentication will replace traditional multi-factor authentication (MFA) by dynamically adjusting security requirements based on evolving threat levels.

Decentralized identity models, built on blockchain and self-sovereign identity (SSI) frameworks, will reshape IAM by giving users greater control over their digital identities while reducing reliance on centralized identity providers. In traditional IAM architectures, identity credentials are stored in enterprise databases or cloud identity services, making them attractive targets for cyberattacks. Decentralized identity eliminates the need for a central authority, allowing users to authenticate using cryptographically verified credentials stored in secure digital wallets. Organizations adopting decentralized identity solutions will benefit from enhanced privacy, reduced risk of credential theft, and improved interoperability across platforms and service providers.

Passwordless authentication will become a standard security practice as organizations move away from reliance on passwords, which are vulnerable to phishing attacks, credential stuffing, and brute-force attempts. Passwordless authentication methods, such as biometrics, security keys, and cryptographic authentication, will replace traditional username-password combinations, reducing the risk of compromised credentials. Identity-centric Zero Trust architectures will integrate passwordless authentication with risk-based access controls, ensuring that users authenticate securely based on device trust, behavioral analytics, and contextual security signals. Advances in WebAuthn and FIDO2 standards will drive the adoption of strong authentication mechanisms that eliminate password-related security risks.

Adaptive and continuous authentication will become essential components of Zero Trust IAM, ensuring that identity verification is not limited to initial login events but continuously validated throughout a session. Static authentication mechanisms allow attackers to exploit session hijacking, stolen tokens, and persistent access privileges. Continuous authentication uses behavioral biometrics, keystroke dynamics, and session analytics to verify user identity dynamically. If a user's behavior deviates from their normal patterns—such as typing inconsistencies, unusual navigation habits, or erratic mouse movements—the system can require additional authentication, limit access, or terminate the session. This approach enhances security while minimizing friction for legitimate users.

Zero Trust IAM will expand beyond human identities to secure machine identities, API access, and service-to-service communications. As organizations adopt cloud-native architectures, DevOps pipelines, and microservices, securing non-human identities becomes increasingly critical. Machine identities, including service accounts, API tokens, and cryptographic certificates, are frequently targeted by attackers seeking to exploit automated workflows. Future IAM solutions will enforce strict access policies for machine identities, integrating identity-based Zero Trust principles with API security gateways, identity federation, and automated secrets management. Just-in-time (JIT) access provisioning for machine identities will minimize standing privileges, ensuring that service-to-service interactions are secure and time-bound.

Cloud IAM innovations will continue to redefine Zero Trust security by integrating identity-based access policies with multi-cloud environments, hybrid infrastructures, and edge computing. Organizations operating across multiple cloud providers face challenges in maintaining consistent access controls, enforcing least privilege, and securing cloud workloads. Future IAM solutions will provide unified identity governance across AWS, Azure, Google Cloud, and private cloud environments, ensuring seamless authentication and access policy enforcement. AI-driven cloud IAM will automate privilege management, detect identity-related misconfigurations, and enforce compliance with real-time security assessments. Cloud-based identity providers will enable zero-touch provisioning, ensuring that users and devices gain access dynamically based on contextual trust levels.

Identity threat detection and response (ITDR) will emerge as a core component of Zero Trust IAM, providing real-time threat intelligence and automated incident response capabilities. Attackers increasingly target IAM systems through credential theft, privilege abuse, and identity-based attacks. Future ITDR solutions will integrate with SIEM platforms, UEBA analytics, and Zero Trust enforcement mechanisms to detect anomalous access behaviors, flag compromised accounts, and automatically revoke access in response to security threats. AI-powered ITDR will proactively identify patterns of identity compromise, preventing lateral movement and unauthorized access before attackers can exploit IAM vulnerabilities.

Zero Trust governance and compliance automation will play a vital role in ensuring regulatory adherence and security best practices across enterprise IAM environments. Compliance requirements such as GDPR, HIPAA, PCI DSS, and NIST 800-53 mandate strict identity verification, audit logging, and access control policies. Future IAM solutions will automate compliance enforcement by continuously monitoring identity policies, detecting access violations, and generating real-time audit reports. AI-driven compliance analytics will predict security gaps, recommend policy adjustments, and enforce security baselines, reducing manual oversight and improving regulatory adherence.

User experience will be a major focus in the evolution of Zero Trust IAM, ensuring that security controls do not create unnecessary friction for legitimate users. Future identity verification methods will balance security with usability by leveraging contextual authentication, AI-driven access recommendations, and risk-aware adaptive policies. Organizations will implement frictionless authentication experiences, such as mobile-based identity verification, behavioral authentication, and transparent risk-based access decisions, reducing disruptions while maintaining Zero Trust security principles. Personalized access policies will dynamically adjust based on user role, location, and historical behavior, ensuring that security measures align with business needs without compromising protection.

The future of Zero Trust and IAM innovations will be shaped by AI-driven security analytics, decentralized identity models, passwordless authentication, continuous authentication, and advanced identity governance. As organizations embrace cloud-first strategies, digital transformation, and hybrid workforces, IAM will become the foundation of enterprise security, ensuring that identity remains the central control point in Zero Trust architectures. By integrating automation, AI, and risk-based security policies, the next generation of Zero Trust IAM will provide adaptive, scalable, and intelligent identity protection against evolving cyber threats.

Least Privilege and Third-Party Access Management

Least privilege access is a fundamental security principle that ensures users, applications, and systems have only the minimum permissions necessary to perform their tasks. In modern enterprises, third-party vendors, contractors, and business partners often require access to critical systems, cloud applications, and sensitive data. Managing third-party access while enforcing least privilege is a significant challenge, as excessive permissions, lack of visibility, and inadequate controls can lead to security risks, data breaches, and compliance violations. Organizations must implement robust third-party access management strategies that align with least privilege principles to minimize attack surfaces, prevent unauthorized access, and ensure secure collaboration.

Third-party access introduces security risks due to the varying security postures of external vendors. Unlike internal employees, third-party users may not follow the same cybersecurity protocols, use unmanaged devices, or access systems from untrusted networks. Many data breaches have occurred due to compromised vendor credentials or inadequate access controls that allowed attackers to exploit third-party relationships. Enforcing least privilege ensures that third-party users have access only to the specific applications and data necessary for their roles, reducing the risk of credential abuse and insider threats.

Identity and Access Management (IAM) plays a crucial role in enforcing least privilege for third-party users by implementing strong authentication, granular authorization policies, and continuous monitoring. Organizations must establish a centralized IAM framework that integrates with third-party identity providers, ensuring that vendors authenticate securely before accessing enterprise resources. Multi-Factor Authentication (MFA) is essential for securing third-party accounts, preventing unauthorized access even if credentials are compromised. Adaptive authentication enhances security by dynamically adjusting authentication requirements based on user risk profiles, device security posture, and contextual access conditions.

Just-in-Time (JIT) access provisioning is a critical component of least privilege enforcement for third-party users, granting temporary access only when required. Many organizations assign persistent credentials to vendors, increasing the risk of account misuse and unauthorized access. JIT access eliminates standing privileges by provisioning access dynamically for a predefined period, ensuring that third-party accounts cannot be exploited outside of approved sessions. Privileged Access Management (PAM) solutions enforce JIT access for high-risk third-party accounts, requiring approval workflows before granting administrative permissions to external vendors.

Role-Based Access Control (RBAC) and Attribute-Based Access Control (ABAC) provide structured access management for third-party users, ensuring that permissions align with their job functions. RBAC assigns access based on predefined roles, ensuring that vendors receive only the necessary permissions for their specific tasks. ABAC enhances least privilege by incorporating contextual attributes, such as device trust, location, and security posture, before granting access. If a third-party contractor attempts to log in from an unmanaged device or an untrusted network, ABAC policies can enforce additional authentication requirements or restrict access altogether.

Zero Trust Network Access (ZTNA) replaces traditional VPN-based third-party access models, ensuring that vendors do not receive broad network access once authenticated. VPNs grant excessive privileges, allowing third-party users to move laterally within enterprise networks if compromised. ZTNA enforces identity-aware access controls, restricting third-party access to specific applications and services based on real-time verification. If a vendor needs to troubleshoot a cloud environment, ZTNA ensures that access is granted only to the necessary cloud resources, preventing unauthorized access to internal systems and sensitive data.

Third-party identity federation streamlines access management by integrating external identity providers with enterprise IAM platforms. Instead of creating separate accounts for each vendor, organizations implement Single Sign-On (SSO) and federated authentication to allow vendors to use their existing credentials securely. Identity federation reduces the risk of credential sprawl, improves access visibility, and ensures that third-party users adhere to the same authentication policies as internal employees. By enforcing federated authentication, organizations maintain centralized control over third-party access while reducing administrative overhead.

Continuous monitoring and auditing of third-party activities are essential for enforcing least privilege and detecting potential security risks. Many organizations lack visibility into how third-party users interact with enterprise systems, increasing the risk of unauthorized access and data exposure. Security Information and Event Management (SIEM) solutions, combined with User and Entity Behavior Analytics (UEBA), detect anomalies in third-party access patterns, identifying suspicious behavior such as excessive data downloads, privilege escalation attempts, or access from high-risk locations. Automated security alerts ensure that unauthorized activities are promptly investigated and remediated.

Data Loss Prevention (DLP) policies prevent unauthorized sharing or exfiltration of sensitive data by third-party users. Many vendors require access to corporate data for collaboration, but excessive permissions can lead to accidental or intentional data leaks. DLP solutions enforce data protection policies, blocking unauthorized file transfers, encrypting sensitive information, and restricting third-party access to confidential documents. Cloud Access Security Brokers (CASBs) provide additional security for third-party interactions with cloud applications, ensuring that vendors cannot expose sensitive data through misconfigured cloud settings or unsecured file-sharing platforms.

Regulatory compliance frameworks, such as GDPR, HIPAA, PCI DSS, and ISO 27001, mandate strict access controls for third-party users to prevent unauthorized access to sensitive information. Organizations must implement least privilege policies to meet compliance requirements, ensuring that vendors have only the permissions necessary for contractual obligations. Automated compliance reporting and audit logging provide visibility into third-party access activities, ensuring that organizations maintain regulatory adherence while reducing legal and security risks.

Revoking third-party access when contracts end or projects are completed is a critical component of least privilege enforcement. Many organizations fail to deprovision vendor accounts promptly, leaving inactive credentials exposed to potential exploitation. Automated identity lifecycle management ensures that third-party accounts are disabled immediately after they are no longer needed. Periodic access reviews validate that vendor permissions remain appropriate, preventing privilege creep and reducing the risk of unauthorized long-term access.

AI-driven security automation enhances third-party access management by dynamically adjusting access policies based on risk assessments, threat intelligence, and behavioral analytics. AI-driven IAM solutions detect anomalies in third-party access requests, enforcing step-up authentication for high-risk transactions and automatically revoking privileges when suspicious activities are detected. Automated access controls reduce the burden on security teams while ensuring that third-party users maintain secure and compliant access to enterprise resources.

Organizations must integrate least privilege principles with third-party access management to minimize security risks, prevent data breaches, and maintain compliance with regulatory mandates. By implementing JIT access provisioning, ZTNA, continuous monitoring, and AI-driven security automation, organizations ensure that vendors, contractors, and business partners access enterprise resources securely while reducing the attack surface. As cyber threats targeting third-party relationships continue to evolve, enforcing least privilege for external users remains a critical security strategy for protecting sensitive data and maintaining trust in digital ecosystems.

Continuous Access Evaluation and Zero Trust Frameworks

Continuous Access Evaluation (CAE) is a critical component of modern Zero Trust security frameworks, ensuring that access decisions are dynamically enforced based on real-time risk assessments, user behavior, and changing security conditions. Traditional access control models rely on static authentication events, where users gain access to corporate systems after successfully logging in. However, once authenticated, these models often fail to revalidate user sessions, allowing attackers to exploit stolen credentials or hijacked sessions. Continuous Access Evaluation addresses this limitation by implementing real-time, identity-aware security policies that assess and enforce access decisions throughout a session.

Zero Trust security frameworks operate on the principle that no user, device, or application should be inherently trusted. Every access request must be continuously verified based on contextual risk signals, including login location, device security posture, application sensitivity, and behavioral analytics. CAE enhances Zero Trust by ensuring that access permissions are not granted indefinitely but are instead dynamically revalidated at regular intervals or in response to security events. If a user's device becomes compromised, their risk profile changes, or suspicious activity is detected, Zero Trust frameworks enforce adaptive access controls to restrict, challenge, or revoke access in real time.

Identity and Access Management (IAM) platforms integrate CAE with Zero Trust architectures to enforce risk-based authentication and real-time access governance. Traditional IAM solutions rely on single sign-on (SSO) and session-based authentication, which do not account for security changes after the initial login. CAE ensures that IAM policies continuously evaluate risk factors, preventing long-lived authentication sessions from being exploited by attackers. By implementing CAE, organizations can detect session anomalies, enforce step-up authentication when needed, and dynamically terminate access if security risks escalate.

Risk-based authentication is a fundamental aspect of Continuous Access Evaluation, ensuring that access decisions remain aligned with evolving threat conditions. Static authentication mechanisms treat all login attempts equally, regardless of contextual risk. CAE leverages AI-driven security analytics to assess login behavior, access history, and device trust before granting or maintaining access. If an authenticated user attempts to access high-risk applications from an unrecognized location or device, CAE can require additional verification, such as biometric authentication, one-time passcodes, or hardware security tokens. If an account exhibits unusual activity, such as excessive file downloads or privilege escalation attempts, CAE can automatically revoke access or enforce a security review.

Device security posture is another key factor in Continuous Access Evaluation, ensuring that only trusted and compliant endpoints can maintain access to corporate resources. Many cyberattacks exploit vulnerabilities in unpatched devices, outdated operating systems, or unauthorized applications. CAE integrates with Endpoint Detection and Response (EDR) and Mobile Device Management (MDM) solutions to continuously assess device health, checking for security updates, encryption status, and potential malware infections. If a device falls out of compliance, CAE can enforce conditional access policies, restricting access until the security issue is resolved.

Zero Trust Network Access (ZTNA) extends Continuous Access Evaluation to network security by dynamically adjusting access permissions based on identity, session activity, and real-time risk analysis. Unlike traditional VPNs, which provide broad network access once authenticated, ZTNA enforces per-session authentication and policy-based access controls. If a user attempts to access unauthorized resources or their session behavior deviates from expected patterns, ZTNA can trigger reauthentication or isolate the session to prevent lateral movement within the network. CAE ensures that ZTNA policies remain adaptive, responding to emerging threats as they occur.

Cloud security and Software-as-a-Service (SaaS) applications benefit from CAE by enforcing continuous verification of user sessions, preventing unauthorized access due to token theft, credential sharing, or account takeovers. Many SaaS platforms issue long-lived authentication tokens, allowing users to remain signed in indefinitely. Attackers who gain access to stolen tokens can exploit these persistent sessions to bypass authentication controls. CAE mitigates this risk by enforcing real-time access revocation, revalidating authentication tokens at regular intervals, and requiring users to reauthenticate if risk conditions change.

Privileged Access Management (PAM) integrates CAE with Zero Trust frameworks to enforce strict security controls over high-risk administrative accounts. Privileged users, such as IT administrators and cloud engineers, require elevated permissions to manage critical infrastructure. However, attackers frequently target privileged accounts to gain control over enterprise systems. CAE ensures that privileged access is continuously monitored and reassessed based on real-time security signals. If a privileged user attempts to modify security settings, access restricted systems, or exhibit suspicious behavior, CAE policies can enforce additional security measures, such as just-in-time (JIT) access provisioning, session recording, or immediate access termination.

Behavioral analytics and anomaly detection enhance CAE by identifying deviations from normal access patterns, preventing unauthorized access before security breaches occur. AI-driven User and Entity Behavior Analytics (UEBA) analyze authentication attempts, data access patterns, and system interactions to detect high-risk activities. If a user who typically accesses financial reports suddenly attempts to export large amounts of customer data, CAE can trigger automated security responses, such as enforcing step-up authentication, logging the event for security review, or blocking the action entirely. By continuously adapting to user behavior, CAE minimizes the risk of insider threats and compromised accounts.

Compliance and regulatory frameworks mandate continuous access monitoring to ensure data protection and security best practices. Regulations such as GDPR, HIPAA, PCI DSS, and NIST 800-53 require organizations to enforce strict access controls, audit user activities, and prevent unauthorized data exposure. CAE supports compliance efforts by providing continuous authentication validation, real-time security auditing, and automated access revocation in response to security incidents. By integrating CAE with compliance monitoring tools, organizations can maintain regulatory adherence while reducing the risk of identity-related security breaches.

Security automation further enhances Continuous Access Evaluation by enabling real-time policy enforcement and adaptive threat response. AI-driven security orchestration integrates with CAE to automatically adjust access permissions based on evolving risk factors. If a security incident occurs, automated CAE workflows can revoke access, trigger incident response actions, or escalate authentication requirements without manual intervention. By leveraging AI-powered automation, organizations improve security efficiency, reduce administrative workload, and enhance Zero Trust enforcement across enterprise environments.

The integration of Continuous Access Evaluation with Zero Trust frameworks ensures that identity verification, access control, and session monitoring remain adaptive and resilient against emerging threats. By continuously reassessing risk, enforcing conditional access policies, and integrating AI-driven security analytics, CAE strengthens Zero Trust implementations, preventing unauthorized access while maintaining a seamless user experience. As cyber threats evolve, organizations must adopt CAE-driven Zero Trust architectures to secure enterprise identities, protect sensitive data, and enforce real-time security policies across cloud, network, and endpoint environments.

Zero Trust and Software-Defined Perimeters (SDP)

Zero Trust security models eliminate implicit trust by continuously verifying identity, enforcing least privilege access, and dynamically adjusting security policies based on real-time risk assessments. Software-Defined Perimeters (SDP) align with Zero Trust principles by replacing traditional network security models with identity-centric, micro-segmented access controls. Unlike legacy security architectures that rely on perimeter-based defenses, SDP creates an invisible, software-defined boundary around applications and resources, ensuring that only authenticated and authorized users can establish network connections.

Traditional network security models assume that users and devices inside the corporate perimeter can be trusted. However, as organizations adopt cloud computing, remote work, and hybrid IT infrastructures, perimeter-based security is no longer sufficient to prevent unauthorized access. Attackers frequently exploit VPN vulnerabilities, misconfigured firewalls, and exposed network services to gain unauthorized entry into corporate environments. SDP eliminates these risks by dynamically provisioning secure connections based on Zero Trust principles, ensuring that users and devices can only access specific applications without exposing the broader network.

SDP operates on a deny-all-by-default model, meaning that resources remain invisible until authentication and authorization policies validate the user and device. Unlike traditional VPNs, which grant users broad network access once authenticated, SDP enforces per-session authentication and least privilege access, ensuring that users can only interact with the specific resources they are authorized to use. This eliminates the risk of lateral movement within the network, preventing attackers from accessing critical infrastructure even if they compromise a legitimate user's credentials.

Identity and Access Management (IAM) plays a crucial role in SDP by enforcing strict authentication and authorization policies before establishing network connections. SDP solutions integrate with IAM platforms to verify user identities through multi-factor authentication (MFA), biometric authentication, and risk-based access controls. By continuously evaluating contextual risk factors—such as login location, device security posture, and authentication history—SDP ensures that only trusted users can access sensitive applications. If a user's risk level increases due to suspicious behavior, SDP can enforce step-up authentication, restrict access, or terminate the session entirely.

Micro-segmentation is a key advantage of SDP, ensuring that network access is restricted based on identity, device trust, and application-specific security policies. Traditional network segmentation relies on VLANs, firewalls, and static IP-based access controls, which can be complex to manage and prone to misconfigurations. SDP enforces dynamic micro-segmentation by creating one-to-one encrypted connections between users and applications, preventing unauthorized access to other network resources. If an attacker compromises an endpoint, SDP prevents them from scanning the network, discovering services, or moving laterally to exploit other systems.

Zero Trust Network Access (ZTNA) and SDP share fundamental principles, but SDP provides additional security enhancements by completely hiding network resources from unauthorized users. Traditional ZTNA solutions enforce identity-based access controls but still expose applications to discovery by unauthorized entities. SDP eliminates this exposure by implementing application cloaking, ensuring that unauthorized users cannot detect the existence of protected services. Even if attackers attempt to probe the network, they receive no response, reducing the attack surface and mitigating reconnaissance-based threats.

SDP enhances cloud security by providing secure, identity-driven access to cloud-based applications without exposing them to the internet. Many organizations struggle with securing multi-cloud environments due to inconsistent access controls, misconfigured cloud permissions, and exposed cloud APIs. SDP ensures that cloud workloads remain hidden from unauthorized access by establishing secure, ephemeral connections based on user identity and security policies. If an unauthorized user attempts to access a cloud application, SDP denies the connection before any network traffic reaches the resource, reducing the risk of cloud-based attacks.

Remote workforces benefit significantly from SDP, as it provides secure, seamless access to enterprise applications without relying on legacy VPNs. Traditional VPNs introduce security risks by providing full network access once authentication is successful, increasing the risk of insider threats, credential theft, and ransomware propagation. SDP eliminates these risks by provisioning access dynamically based on Zero Trust principles, ensuring that remote employees only connect to the specific applications they need. By integrating with endpoint security solutions, SDP also ensures that remote devices meet compliance requirements before establishing a secure session.

Privileged Access Management (PAM) integrates with SDP to secure administrative accounts and high-risk users. Privileged accounts, such as IT administrators and DevOps engineers, require access to critical infrastructure and cloud environments, making them prime targets for cyberattacks. SDP enforces just-in-time (JIT) privileged access, ensuring that administrative permissions are granted only when necessary and revoked immediately after the task is completed. If a privileged user attempts to access an unauthorized system, SDP automatically blocks the request, preventing privilege escalation attacks.

Continuous monitoring and real-time threat detection strengthen SDP security by identifying and mitigating suspicious activities. Traditional security models rely on periodic audits and static policies, leaving organizations vulnerable to evolving cyber threats. SDP solutions integrate with Security Information and Event Management (SIEM) platforms and User and Entity Behavior Analytics (UEBA) to detect anomalies in authentication patterns, access attempts, and session behaviors. If SDP detects unusual activity, such as multiple failed authentication attempts, unauthorized privilege escalations, or unexpected data transfers, it can trigger automated security responses, such as terminating sessions, enforcing reauthentication, or alerting security teams.

Regulatory compliance frameworks, including GDPR, HIPAA, PCI DSS, and NIST 800-207, mandate strict access control policies to prevent unauthorized access to sensitive data. SDP aligns with these compliance requirements by enforcing identity-driven access policies, encrypting all network connections, and maintaining detailed audit logs of authentication events. Organizations implementing SDP benefit from enhanced compliance visibility, automated policy enforcement, and reduced risk of access control violations. By integrating SDP with compliance reporting tools, organizations can demonstrate adherence to regulatory mandates while improving overall security posture.

Artificial intelligence (AI) and automation further enhance SDP security by dynamically adjusting access policies based on real-time risk assessments. AI-driven identity analytics continuously analyze user behavior, device telemetry, and threat intelligence to detect high-risk access attempts. If AI detects a compromised account attempting to access protected applications, SDP can automatically enforce adaptive access controls, requiring additional authentication, restricting privileges, or revoking access entirely. By leveraging AI-powered automation, organizations enhance SDP security while reducing administrative complexity.

SDP provides a scalable, identity-driven security framework that aligns with Zero Trust principles, eliminating implicit trust, enforcing least privilege access, and securing cloud, remote, and privileged access environments. By dynamically provisioning network connections, implementing micro-segmentation, and integrating continuous monitoring, SDP minimizes the attack surface and prevents unauthorized access to sensitive applications and data. As organizations continue to adopt cloud-based architectures and hybrid work models, SDP remains a foundational component of Zero Trust security, ensuring that users and devices only access what they need while protecting enterprise assets from evolving cyber threats.

Securing Machine Identities with Least Privilege

Machine identities play a crucial role in modern IT environments, enabling secure communication between applications, cloud services, containers, APIs, and automated processes. As organizations adopt cloud computing, DevOps workflows, and microservices architectures, the number of machine identities grows exponentially. Unlike human users, machine identities do not have direct oversight and are often overlooked in security strategies. Enforcing least privilege for machine identities ensures that these non-human entities operate with minimal permissions, reducing the risk of unauthorized access, privilege escalation, and credential compromise.

Traditional Identity and Access Management (IAM) solutions were designed primarily for human identities, but as automation and machine-to-machine communication increase, securing machine identities becomes a critical security challenge. Many organizations fail to manage service accounts, API keys, cryptographic certificates, and container identities effectively, leading to excessive privileges and security vulnerabilities. Machine identities are often granted persistent and broad access to resources, allowing attackers to exploit misconfigurations, steal credentials, or hijack services. By applying least privilege principles, organizations ensure that machine identities only receive the permissions necessary for specific tasks, minimizing security risks and preventing unauthorized system interactions.

Service accounts are widely used to facilitate automated processes and integrations between enterprise applications. However, these accounts are often configured with excessive privileges, granting them access to multiple systems and sensitive data repositories. Many service accounts use static passwords or API tokens that remain unchanged for extended periods, making them a prime target for attackers. Enforcing least privilege for service accounts involves auditing existing permissions, removing unnecessary access, and implementing just-in-time (JIT) access provisioning. Organizations should also enforce credential rotation, ensuring that service account credentials are updated periodically to mitigate the risk of compromise.

API security is another critical aspect of managing machine identities with least privilege. APIs enable seamless integration between cloud services, microservices, and third-party applications, but they also introduce security risks if not properly managed. API keys and OAuth tokens are often overprivileged, allowing unrestricted access to backend services. Attackers frequently exploit exposed API credentials to launch attacks, exfiltrate data, or gain unauthorized control over enterprise applications. Organizations must enforce fine-grained access controls for API identities, ensuring that each API interaction is authenticated, authorized, and monitored. Implementing Role-Based Access Control (RBAC) and Attribute-Based Access Control (ABAC) ensures that APIs can only perform approved operations, reducing the risk of privilege abuse.

Cloud workloads and containerized applications require strong identity management practices to prevent unauthorized access and lateral movement within cloud environments. Cloud IAM solutions, such as AWS IAM, Azure Active Directory, and Google Cloud IAM, allow organizations to define identity-based policies that enforce least privilege for machine identities. Misconfigured cloud identities often lead to excessive permissions, allowing compromised virtual machines,

Kubernetes pods, or serverless functions to access sensitive resources. By implementing least privilege, organizations restrict machine identities to only the services and data they require, reducing the attack surface and mitigating cloud-based security risks.

Privileged Access Management (PAM) solutions extend least privilege enforcement to machine identities by securing administrative credentials, SSH keys, and automation scripts. Many DevOps workflows rely on hardcoded credentials in configuration files, CI/CD pipelines, and infrastructure-as-code (IaC) templates, increasing the risk of credential leaks. PAM solutions provide secure vaulting and automated credential rotation, ensuring that machine identities do not retain unnecessary privileges or expose sensitive authentication secrets. By integrating PAM with IAM policies, organizations enforce strict access controls while enabling secure machine-to-machine authentication.

Zero Trust security models reinforce least privilege for machine identities by requiring continuous authentication, authorization, and real-time security verification. Unlike traditional security models that assume trusted network zones, Zero Trust ensures that machine identities must always authenticate before accessing resources. Machine identity authentication mechanisms include Mutual TLS (mTLS), certificate-based authentication, and cryptographic attestation. Implementing Zero Trust Network Access (ZTNA) for machine identities prevents unauthorized systems from communicating with enterprise services, ensuring that only verified workloads can access protected environments.

Encryption and secure key management play a vital role in protecting machine identities and enforcing least privilege. Many organizations rely on cryptographic keys for secure data transmission, digital signatures, and workload authentication. However, improperly managed encryption keys can lead to security breaches if they are exposed, misconfigured, or stored in unsecured locations. Organizations should implement enterprise-grade key management solutions, such as AWS KMS, Azure Key Vault, or HashiCorp Vault, to enforce strict access controls over cryptographic assets. By applying least privilege, organizations ensure that only authorized machine identities can access encryption keys, reducing the risk of unauthorized decryption or key misuse.

Continuous monitoring and anomaly detection enhance least privilege enforcement for machine identities by identifying suspicious behavior, privilege misuse, and unauthorized access attempts. Security Information and Event Management (SIEM) platforms and User and Entity Behavior Analytics (UEBA) solutions analyze machine identity interactions, detecting deviations from normal patterns. If a machine identity suddenly requests access to unauthorized resources, exhibits excessive authentication failures, or initiates large-scale data transfers, security teams can investigate and enforce corrective actions. Automated threat detection mechanisms ensure that machine identities operate within approved security policies while preventing potential breaches.

Identity governance frameworks provide structured policies for managing machine identities throughout their lifecycle, ensuring that least privilege is consistently applied. Many organizations lack visibility into the lifecycle of service accounts, API credentials, and automation tokens, leading to security gaps and abandoned credentials. Identity governance solutions automate access reviews, enforce compliance policies, and provide audit trails for machine identity activities. By periodically reviewing machine identity permissions, organizations eliminate unnecessary access, prevent privilege creep, and enforce security best practices across hybrid and multi-cloud environments.

Regulatory compliance mandates strict identity management and access control policies for machine identities, requiring organizations to enforce least privilege to meet security standards. Regulations such as GDPR, HIPAA, PCI DSS, and NIST 800-53 emphasize the importance of protecting automated workflows, securing cloud identities, and preventing unauthorized access. Organizations that fail to manage machine identities securely risk non-compliance penalties, data breaches, and operational disruptions. By implementing automated identity governance, least privilege enforcement, and continuous access monitoring, organizations ensure compliance with regulatory requirements while strengthening machine identity security.

AI-driven security automation enhances least privilege enforcement by dynamically adjusting access policies, detecting high-risk machine identity behaviors, and responding to security threats in real time. Machine learning models analyze historical identity patterns, identifying potential vulnerabilities, excessive permissions, and privilege escalation attempts. AI-driven IAM solutions automate least privilege enforcement, revoking unnecessary permissions, adjusting API access policies, and rotating service credentials based on real-time security insights. By leveraging AI-powered automation, organizations enhance machine identity security while reducing administrative overhead and minimizing human error.

Securing machine identities with least privilege is essential for preventing unauthorized access, minimizing attack surfaces, and ensuring compliance with security best practices. By enforcing strict IAM policies, implementing Zero Trust authentication, leveraging PAM solutions, and continuously monitoring machine identity interactions, organizations protect critical systems from identity-based threats. As automation, cloud services, and API-driven architectures continue to expand, securing machine identities with least privilege remains a foundational component of enterprise security strategy.

Behavioral Analytics for Identity Risk Management

Behavioral analytics is a critical component of identity risk management, enabling organizations to detect anomalous user behavior, prevent unauthorized access, and mitigate insider threats. Traditional security models rely on static authentication mechanisms, such as usernames and passwords, to verify user identities. However, attackers frequently compromise credentials through phishing, brute-force attacks, and social engineering tactics, allowing them to bypass traditional authentication controls. Behavioral analytics enhances identity risk management by continuously monitoring user activities, establishing behavioral baselines, and identifying deviations that may indicate security threats.

Identity and Access Management (IAM) systems integrate behavioral analytics to assess identity risk dynamically, reducing reliance on static authentication methods. Instead of granting persistent access after a single login event, IAM platforms analyze user interactions, device characteristics, and access patterns to enforce adaptive security policies. If a user exhibits behavior inconsistent with their typical usage patterns—such as accessing sensitive data from an unusual location or logging in from multiple devices simultaneously—behavioral analytics can trigger step-up authentication, restrict access, or notify security teams for further investigation.

Machine learning and artificial intelligence (AI) play a crucial role in behavioral analytics, allowing identity risk management systems to analyze vast amounts of user activity data and detect hidden patterns indicative of malicious intent. AI-driven behavioral analytics models continuously learn from user interactions, refining risk assessments over time to improve accuracy and reduce false positives. By analyzing login times, keystroke dynamics, browsing habits, and application usage patterns, AI models differentiate between legitimate user activity and potential account compromise attempts.

User and Entity Behavior Analytics (UEBA) solutions extend behavioral analytics beyond individual users to monitor the activities of applications, systems, and privileged accounts. Many cyberattacks involve compromised service accounts or insider threats where attackers misuse legitimate credentials to evade detection. UEBA solutions analyze entity behavior across IT environments, identifying unusual access requests, privilege escalation attempts, and unauthorized data transfers. If a service account suddenly initiates high-volume data extractions or accesses systems outside its normal scope, behavioral analytics can trigger automated security responses to contain the threat.

Risk-based authentication (RBA) leverages behavioral analytics to dynamically adjust authentication requirements based on real-time risk assessments. Instead of treating all authentication attempts equally, RBA assigns a risk score to each login event, determining whether additional verification is required. For example, if a user logs in from their usual corporate device and office location, the system may grant access with minimal friction. However, if the same user attempts to log in from an unrecognized device or a foreign country, RBA can enforce multi-factor authentication (MFA) or restrict access until the identity is verified.

Privileged Access Management (PAM) benefits from behavioral analytics by detecting anomalous activities associated with high-risk administrative accounts. Privileged users, such as IT administrators and cloud engineers, have elevated access to critical infrastructure, making them prime targets for cyberattacks. Behavioral analytics continuously monitors privileged account interactions, detecting deviations from normal usage patterns. If an administrator suddenly modifies firewall rules, exports large volumes of sensitive data, or accesses systems outside their designated role, PAM solutions can enforce just-in-time (JIT) access controls, trigger real-time security alerts, or revoke permissions to prevent potential breaches.

Insider threat detection is a key application of behavioral analytics in identity risk management, helping organizations identify employees, contractors, or third-party users who may be engaging in malicious activities. Insider threats can be intentional, such as data theft or sabotage, or unintentional, such as accidental data leaks or negligent security practices. Behavioral analytics monitors access logs, document interactions, and email communications to detect patterns of risky behavior. If an employee begins downloading confidential files, attempting to access restricted databases, or engaging in unauthorized communications, security teams can investigate and take preventive actions.

Continuous monitoring and real-time anomaly detection enhance Zero Trust security frameworks by ensuring that identity verification is not a one-time event but an ongoing process. Traditional access control models rely on periodic access reviews and predefined security policies, which may fail to detect evolving threats. Behavioral analytics enables continuous access evaluation, dynamically adjusting access permissions based on changing risk conditions. If a user's risk profile changes during an active session—such as logging in from an unsecured network or accessing unauthorized systems—Zero Trust policies can enforce reauthentication or revoke access immediately.

Cloud security and Software-as-a-Service (SaaS) applications require advanced identity risk management strategies to prevent unauthorized access across distributed environments. Many cloud services rely on persistent authentication tokens, which can be exploited if compromised. Behavioral analytics mitigates this risk by continuously assessing session behavior, identifying anomalies, and enforcing conditional access policies. If a cloud user suddenly starts exporting large volumes of data, modifying security configurations, or accessing privileged resources outside their role, security automation can block the activity and require additional identity verification.

Regulatory compliance mandates strict identity monitoring and access controls to protect sensitive data and prevent unauthorized access. Regulations such as GDPR, HIPAA, PCI DSS, and NIST 800-53 require organizations to implement continuous identity verification, audit logging, and anomaly detection to secure personal and financial information. Behavioral analytics helps organizations comply with these regulations by providing real-time identity risk assessments, automating compliance reporting, and enforcing policy-based access restrictions. Security teams use behavioral analytics insights to generate audit logs, detect policy violations, and ensure compliance with industry standards.

AI-driven security automation enhances identity risk management by enabling proactive threat detection and response. Traditional security models rely on predefined rules and static policies, which may not adapt to emerging cyber threats. AI-driven behavioral analytics continuously refines risk models based on real-world attack patterns, improving the ability to detect sophisticated identity-based threats. Automated security workflows integrate with IAM platforms, enabling organizations to revoke compromised credentials, enforce security patches, or initiate incident response actions in real time.

As identity threats continue to evolve, organizations must adopt behavioral analytics to strengthen identity risk management, enforce Zero Trust principles, and prevent unauthorized access. By leveraging AI-driven security intelligence, continuous authentication, and real-time anomaly detection, organizations reduce identity-related security risks while maintaining seamless user experiences. Integrating behavioral analytics with IAM, UEBA, PAM, and cloud security frameworks ensures that identity protection remains adaptive, intelligent, and resilient against modern cyber threats.

Zero Trust for Multi-Cloud Environments

Zero Trust is a security framework that eliminates implicit trust and continuously verifies users, devices, and workloads before granting access to resources. In multi-cloud environments, where organizations leverage multiple cloud providers such as AWS, Microsoft Azure, and Google Cloud, implementing Zero Trust is critical to securing identities, applications, and data across distributed infrastructures. Traditional perimeter-based security models are ineffective in cloud-native architectures, where workloads, APIs, and services interact dynamically across different cloud platforms. Zero Trust provides a unified security approach that enforces least privilege access, identity-based controls, and continuous monitoring across multi-cloud environments.

Identity and Access Management (IAM) is foundational to Zero Trust in multi-cloud environments, ensuring that only authenticated and authorized users and workloads can access cloud resources. Each cloud provider offers native IAM services, such as AWS IAM, Azure Active Directory (Azure AD), and Google Cloud IAM, but managing identities across multiple cloud platforms presents security and operational challenges. Organizations must implement identity federation, Single

Sign-On (SSO), and centralized IAM policies to ensure consistent authentication, authorization, and privilege management across all cloud providers. Integrating IAM with Zero Trust frameworks ensures that access decisions are dynamic and context-aware, reducing the risk of credential compromise and unauthorized access.

Multi-Factor Authentication (MFA) enhances Zero Trust security by requiring additional verification beyond passwords for cloud access. Password-based authentication alone is insufficient in multi-cloud environments, where attackers frequently exploit weak credentials through phishing, brute-force attacks, and credential stuffing. Zero Trust enforces adaptive MFA based on risk levels, requiring additional authentication factors when users access high-risk cloud workloads, attempt privilege escalation, or log in from untrusted locations. Cloud-native MFA solutions integrate with IAM platforms, ensuring that authentication policies remain consistent across all cloud environments.

Least privilege access is a key Zero Trust principle that restricts users, applications, and workloads to the minimum permissions necessary to perform their tasks. Many organizations struggle with overprivileged cloud IAM roles, where users and services retain unnecessary permissions long after they are needed. Implementing Role-Based Access Control (RBAC) and Attribute-Based Access Control (ABAC) ensures that access is dynamically assigned based on job functions, contextual risk factors, and security policies. Just-in-Time (JIT) access provisioning further strengthens least privilege enforcement by granting temporary permissions only when required, reducing the attack surface and limiting the impact of compromised accounts.

Zero Trust Network Access (ZTNA) replaces traditional VPN-based security models in multi-cloud environments, ensuring that cloud workloads and applications remain protected from unauthorized access. Unlike VPNs, which provide broad network access once authenticated, ZTNA enforces granular access controls based on identity, device trust, and real-time security posture. By integrating ZTNA with cloud-native security solutions, organizations prevent unauthorized lateral movement, restrict access to sensitive cloud workloads, and enforce continuous verification before establishing connections to cloud applications.

Micro-segmentation enhances Zero Trust security in multi-cloud environments by isolating workloads and restricting communication based on identity-aware policies. Traditional network segmentation methods, such as firewalls and VLANs, are insufficient in cloud environments where applications, containers, and microservices communicate dynamically. Cloud-native micro-segmentation enforces identity-based security controls, ensuring that workloads can only interact with authorized services and preventing unauthorized east-west traffic between cloud instances. By implementing software-defined networking (SDN) and identity-aware firewalls, organizations reduce the risk of cloud-based attacks and prevent attackers from exploiting misconfigured security groups and open network ports.

Cloud Security Posture Management (CSPM) aligns with Zero Trust by continuously monitoring multi-cloud environments for misconfigurations, excessive permissions, and policy violations. Many cloud security breaches result from misconfigured storage buckets, overprivileged IAM roles, or exposed APIs. CSPM solutions provide real-time visibility into cloud security risks, enforcing Zero Trust policies that automatically remediate misconfigurations and enforce least privilege access controls. By integrating CSPM with Zero Trust frameworks, organizations ensure that security policies remain consistent across all cloud platforms, reducing the risk of data exposure and unauthorized access.

Privileged Access Management (PAM) extends Zero Trust security to high-risk administrative accounts and cloud management interfaces. Cloud administrators, DevOps engineers, and security teams require elevated privileges to manage infrastructure, but these privileged accounts are prime targets for cyberattacks. PAM enforces strict access controls for privileged users, requiring JIT access provisioning, session monitoring, and continuous authentication. By integrating PAM with Zero Trust, organizations prevent privilege escalation attacks, unauthorized configuration changes, and insider threats in multi-cloud environments.

API security is a critical aspect of Zero Trust in multi-cloud environments, as cloud applications and services rely heavily on APIs for communication and automation. Many cloud security breaches occur due to exposed or unsecured APIs that allow unauthorized access to cloud workloads. Zero Trust enforces strong authentication, authorization, and encryption for API interactions, ensuring that only verified identities can access cloud APIs. Implementing API gateways, rate limiting, and identity-aware API policies prevents API abuse, reduces attack surfaces, and mitigates risks associated with exposed cloud endpoints.

Continuous monitoring and threat detection strengthen Zero Trust in multi-cloud environments by providing real-time insights into identity risks, access anomalies, and cloud security incidents. Traditional security models rely on periodic audits and static policies, which fail to detect evolving threats in dynamic cloud infrastructures. Security Information and Event Management (SIEM) platforms, combined with User and Entity Behavior Analytics (UEBA), analyze cloud access logs, detect deviations from normal behavior, and trigger automated security responses. If a cloud user exhibits suspicious activity, such as accessing unauthorized resources or attempting privilege escalation, Zero Trust policies can enforce real-time remediation, such as requiring reauthentication, restricting access, or terminating the session.

Compliance and regulatory requirements necessitate strict security controls for multi-cloud environments, ensuring that organizations meet industry standards such as GDPR, HIPAA, PCI DSS, and NIST 800-53. Many regulatory frameworks mandate strong authentication, least privilege access, and continuous security monitoring to protect sensitive cloud data. Zero Trust helps organizations maintain compliance by enforcing automated access controls, logging all identity interactions, and providing audit trails for cloud security events. Cloud-native compliance automation tools integrate with Zero

Trust frameworks, ensuring that security policies align with regulatory mandates while reducing administrative overhead.

Artificial intelligence (AI) and security automation enhance Zero Trust implementation in multi-cloud environments by dynamically adjusting access policies, detecting high-risk activities, and enforcing real-time security responses. AI-driven identity analytics continuously assess user behavior, device trust levels, and cloud security configurations, identifying potential risks before they escalate into security incidents. Automated remediation workflows revoke excessive permissions, enforce security patches, and adapt Zero Trust policies based on real-time threat intelligence. By leveraging AI-driven automation, organizations enhance Zero Trust enforcement while improving operational efficiency in multi-cloud environments.

Zero Trust provides a comprehensive security framework for multi-cloud environments, ensuring that access decisions are identity-driven, continuously monitored, and dynamically adjusted based on risk. By integrating IAM, ZTNA, micro-segmentation, API security, and AI-driven threat detection, organizations reduce attack surfaces, prevent unauthorized access, and maintain compliance across cloud platforms. As cloud adoption accelerates, implementing Zero Trust in multi-cloud environments remains essential for securing enterprise workloads, protecting sensitive data, and mitigating evolving cyber threats.

The Role of Identity Proofing in Zero Trust

Identity proofing is a fundamental component of the Zero Trust security model, ensuring that users, devices, and applications are who they claim to be before granting access to systems, networks, and data. Traditional authentication methods, such as usernames and passwords, are no longer sufficient to verify identity due to the increasing sophistication of cyber threats, including phishing attacks, credential theft, and social engineering tactics. Zero Trust eliminates implicit trust and requires continuous verification, starting with strong identity proofing mechanisms that establish trust at the point of initial enrollment and throughout the identity lifecycle.

Identity proofing involves validating a user's identity using multiple verification factors, such as government-issued documents, biometric data, and real-time identity verification techniques. Unlike simple authentication, which only validates a user based on known credentials, identity proofing ensures that the claimed identity corresponds to a real person with verifiable attributes. In the context of Zero Trust, identity proofing acts as the first security checkpoint before granting access to corporate resources, preventing identity fraud and unauthorized access.

Multi-factor authentication (MFA) enhances identity proofing by requiring additional verification methods beyond passwords. However, MFA alone is not enough if the initial identity verification process is weak. If an attacker successfully enrolls in an organization's system using a stolen or synthetic identity, they can bypass MFA and gain access to sensitive resources. To prevent this, organizations must implement identity proofing measures that validate the authenticity of new accounts before issuing credentials. Document verification, facial recognition, and knowledge-based authentication (KBA) are commonly used identity proofing methods to ensure that users are legitimate before they gain access to enterprise systems.

Digital identity proofing plays a crucial role in remote work environments, where employees, contractors, and third-party vendors authenticate from various locations using different devices. Organizations must establish trust in remote identities before granting access to sensitive applications. Remote identity proofing solutions leverage AI-driven facial recognition, liveness detection, and government ID verification to confirm user identities without requiring physical presence. Zero Trust frameworks integrate these digital identity proofing solutions to ensure that users meet strict verification standards before accessing cloud-based services and enterprise networks.

Zero Trust frameworks enforce identity proofing for both human and non-human entities, including service accounts, IoT devices, and API-based communications. Machine identities, such as digital certificates, cryptographic keys, and API tokens, must also undergo identity proofing to prevent unauthorized access and impersonation attacks. Organizations implement Public Key Infrastructure (PKI) and certificate-based authentication to verify machine identities before allowing them to interact with enterprise resources. By extending identity proofing to both human and machine identities, Zero Trust ensures that all entities accessing a system are continuously validated and monitored.

Behavioral analytics strengthens identity proofing by detecting anomalies in user behavior that may indicate fraudulent identities or compromised accounts. AI-driven identity proofing solutions analyze login patterns, typing speed, mouse movements, and access history to identify inconsistencies in user behavior. If a newly created account exhibits suspicious activity, such as attempting to access high-risk resources immediately after enrollment, Zero Trust policies can trigger additional verification steps or revoke access until the identity is revalidated. Continuous identity proofing ensures that trust is not granted indefinitely but is dynamically reassessed based on evolving risk conditions.

Regulatory compliance frameworks, including GDPR, HIPAA, and NIST 800-63, mandate strict identity proofing requirements to protect sensitive data and prevent unauthorized access. Organizations operating in highly regulated industries must implement strong identity verification processes to ensure compliance with legal and security mandates. Zero Trust aligns with these regulatory requirements by enforcing rigorous identity proofing policies, maintaining audit trails of identity verification events, and applying risk-based authentication to protect critical assets. Automated compliance reporting tools help organizations demonstrate adherence to identity proofing standards while reducing manual verification efforts.

Fraud prevention is a key benefit of identity proofing in Zero Trust environments, preventing attackers from using stolen identities or synthetic accounts to bypass security controls. Synthetic identity fraud, where cybercriminals create fake identities using a combination of real and fabricated information, is a growing threat in financial services, healthcare, and government sectors. Advanced identity proofing solutions use AI-powered document analysis, biometric authentication, and threat intelligence to detect fraudulent accounts before they gain access to enterprise systems. By integrating identity proofing with Zero Trust policies, organizations prevent unauthorized users from exploiting identity-based vulnerabilities.

Privileged Access Management (PAM) integrates identity proofing to ensure that high-risk administrative accounts are subject to enhanced verification before being granted access to critical systems. Privileged users, such as system administrators and cloud engineers, require elevated permissions, making them prime targets for attackers. Zero Trust enforces identity proofing for privileged accounts by requiring re-verification at regular intervals, enforcing strict credential issuance processes, and integrating identity-proofing solutions with PAM workflows. If an administrator attempts to access a sensitive database from an untrusted location, Zero Trust policies can trigger real-time identity revalidation before allowing access.

Zero Trust identity proofing extends beyond initial enrollment, requiring ongoing identity verification throughout the user's lifecycle. Organizations implement lifecycle identity proofing to ensure that employees, contractors, and vendors maintain valid credentials and meet security requirements over time. Regular identity reproofing checks verify that users still require access to enterprise systems and have not been compromised or subjected to identity theft. Automated identity proofing workflows streamline revalidation processes, ensuring that access policies remain aligned with business needs and security requirements.

Cloud security and Software-as-a-Service (SaaS) platforms rely on identity proofing to prevent unauthorized access to enterprise applications. Many organizations adopt identity-as-a-service (IDaaS) solutions that integrate identity proofing with cloud IAM platforms, ensuring that users must undergo strict verification before accessing cloud-based workloads. AI-driven identity proofing solutions enhance Zero Trust security by analyzing identity risks in real time, adapting access policies based on behavioral analytics, and enforcing step-up authentication for high-risk login attempts. Organizations that leverage identity proofing for cloud security mitigate the risk of unauthorized access, credential stuffing, and identity-based attacks.

Artificial intelligence and machine learning enhance identity proofing by continuously improving verification accuracy, detecting identity fraud attempts, and automating risk-based decision-making. AI-driven identity proofing solutions analyze thousands of data points, including biometric traits, document authenticity, and device fingerprints, to verify users with high confidence. As AI algorithms refine identity verification models, Zero Trust security frameworks adapt to emerging threats, ensuring that identity proofing remains effective against evolving cyber risks. By leveraging AI for identity proofing, organizations strengthen authentication processes while reducing friction for legitimate users.

Zero Trust security models rely on robust identity proofing mechanisms to establish trust, prevent identity fraud, and enforce continuous verification. By integrating AI-driven identity proofing solutions, behavioral analytics, and biometric authentication, organizations enhance identity security while mitigating risks associated with credential theft and unauthorized access. As identity threats continue to evolve, Zero Trust identity proofing remains a foundational security control, ensuring that all users, devices, and applications accessing enterprise systems are continuously validated and verified.

Secure Access Service Edge (SASE) and Zero Trust

Secure Access Service Edge (SASE) is a modern cybersecurity framework that integrates network security and wide-area networking

(WAN) with cloud-native security services to provide secure, identity-driven access to applications and data. As organizations adopt cloud-first strategies, remote workforces, and distributed IT environments, traditional network security models become insufficient. Zero Trust, which eliminates implicit trust and enforces continuous authentication and authorization, aligns with SASE principles to provide a comprehensive approach to securing network access, protecting cloud workloads, and ensuring data security across hybrid environments.

Traditional perimeter-based security models rely on centralized data centers, firewalls, and VPNs to protect enterprise resources. However, as applications move to the cloud and users access data from various locations and devices, legacy security architectures introduce bottlenecks, performance issues, and security risks. SASE redefines network security by shifting security controls to the cloud, enforcing Zero Trust principles at the network edge, and enabling secure access based on user identity, device posture, and contextual risk assessments. By integrating SASE with Zero Trust, organizations ensure that every access request is continuously verified and dynamically adjusted based on real-time security intelligence.

Identity and Access Management (IAM) is foundational to SASE, ensuring that users, applications, and devices are authenticated before gaining access to network resources. Unlike traditional security models that grant broad network access once authentication is successful, SASE enforces Zero Trust Network Access (ZTNA), restricting users to specific applications and data based on least privilege access policies. By integrating IAM with SASE, organizations implement strong authentication mechanisms such as Multi-Factor Authentication (MFA), identity federation, and adaptive access controls, ensuring that only authorized entities can connect to enterprise systems.

Zero Trust Network Access (ZTNA) is a core component of SASE, replacing legacy VPNs with identity-driven access controls. VPNs provide excessive access by allowing authenticated users to connect to entire network segments, increasing the risk of lateral movement and insider threats. ZTNA enforces granular access policies, verifying user identity, device compliance, and security posture before granting access to applications. If a user attempts to access a sensitive cloud service from an untrusted device or network, ZTNA can enforce additional authentication requirements, restrict access, or deny the request based on real-time risk assessments.

Cloud security is a critical aspect of SASE, as organizations increasingly rely on Software-as-a-Service (SaaS), Infrastructure-as-a-Service (IaaS), and hybrid cloud environments to support business operations. SASE integrates Cloud Access Security Broker (CASB) solutions to monitor and control cloud access, enforce data protection policies, and detect unauthorized activity. Zero Trust principles ensure that cloud access is continuously validated, preventing unauthorized data sharing, misconfigured cloud permissions, and API security vulnerabilities. By enforcing contextual access controls, organizations reduce the risk of data breaches and cloud-based cyber threats.

Software-Defined Wide Area Networking (SD-WAN) is a key networking component of SASE, providing secure, optimized connectivity for remote users, branch offices, and cloud workloads. Traditional WAN architectures rely on private network connections and centralized security gateways, limiting scalability and performance. SASE integrates SD-WAN with Zero Trust security policies, ensuring that traffic is dynamically routed based on security posture, application sensitivity, and real-time risk assessments. By applying Zero Trust principles to SD-WAN, organizations enforce identity-based routing, encrypt network traffic, and prevent unauthorized access to corporate resources.

Secure Web Gateway (SWG) solutions within SASE enforce Zero Trust policies by inspecting web traffic, blocking malicious content, and preventing data leakage. Many cyberattacks originate from web-based threats, including phishing sites, malware-laden downloads, and domain spoofing attacks. SWG integrates with Zero Trust frameworks to inspect encrypted traffic, apply policy-based access controls, and enforce URL filtering. If a user attempts to access a suspicious website or download unapproved software, SWG policies can block the request, preventing potential security incidents.

Data Loss Prevention (DLP) enhances SASE security by preventing unauthorized data transfers, encrypting sensitive information, and enforcing compliance policies. Traditional security models struggle to monitor and control data flow across cloud applications, SaaS platforms, and remote endpoints. SASE integrates DLP solutions to apply Zero Trust-based security policies, ensuring that sensitive data remains protected regardless of user location or access method. If a user attempts to upload confidential documents to an unapproved cloud storage service, DLP policies can block the action and generate security alerts for investigation.

Threat intelligence and real-time monitoring are essential to SASE and Zero Trust implementations, providing continuous visibility into network activity, user behavior, and emerging security threats. SASE integrates with Security Information and Event Management (SIEM) and User and Entity Behavior Analytics (UEBA) solutions to detect anomalous access patterns, privilege escalation attempts, and potential security breaches. AI-driven analytics enhance threat detection by identifying deviations from normal behavior, triggering automated security responses, and dynamically adjusting Zero Trust policies to mitigate risks.

Endpoint security plays a critical role in SASE, ensuring that devices accessing enterprise resources comply with security policies and meet risk assessment criteria. Many cyberattacks target endpoints through malware infections, credential theft, and unauthorized device access. SASE integrates Endpoint Detection and Response (EDR) solutions to enforce Zero Trust security policies, continuously monitoring device health, detecting security threats, and isolating compromised endpoints. If an endpoint exhibits suspicious activity, SASE policies can automatically restrict network access, quarantine the device, and initiate security remediation actions.

Regulatory compliance mandates strict security controls for network access, data protection, and identity verification. SASE supports compliance with frameworks such as GDPR, HIPAA, PCI DSS, and NIST 800-53 by enforcing Zero Trust policies, encrypting network traffic, and maintaining audit logs of security events. Automated compliance monitoring tools integrated with SASE ensure that organizations meet regulatory requirements while reducing the risk of security violations. By implementing SASE and Zero Trust together, organizations enhance compliance posture, simplify security management, and reduce the burden of manual compliance reporting.

Artificial intelligence (AI) and automation enhance SASE security by dynamically adjusting Zero Trust policies based on evolving threats, real-time risk intelligence, and user behavior analytics. AI-driven security automation enables organizations to detect security incidents faster, enforce adaptive access controls, and respond to cyber threats with minimal human intervention. AI-powered SASE solutions continuously analyze network traffic, identify security anomalies, and apply policy-based controls to prevent unauthorized access and data breaches.

SASE provides a scalable, identity-driven security framework that aligns with Zero Trust principles, ensuring that access to applications, data, and cloud environments is continuously verified and protected. By integrating Zero Trust Network Access, cloud security, SD-WAN, threat intelligence, and AI-driven security automation, SASE enhances network security, prevents unauthorized access, and enables secure remote work and cloud adoption. As cyber threats continue to evolve, SASE and Zero Trust remain essential security strategies for protecting modern enterprise networks, reducing attack surfaces, and ensuring seamless, secure access to digital resources.

Implementing Least Privilege in Kubernetes and Containers

Least privilege is a fundamental security principle that ensures users, processes, and services only have the minimum permissions necessary to perform their functions. In Kubernetes and containerized environments, implementing least privilege is essential to reducing the attack surface, preventing unauthorized access, and mitigating privilege escalation risks. Containers operate in highly dynamic and distributed architectures, making security challenges more complex than in traditional monolithic applications. Applying least privilege principles across Kubernetes clusters, container runtimes, and orchestration mechanisms ensures that workloads remain secure, resilient, and isolated from potential threats.

Kubernetes manages containerized applications using declarative configurations and automated scheduling, but by default, many deployments do not enforce strict security policies. Excessive permissions for Kubernetes pods, service accounts, and API requests can lead to security vulnerabilities, allowing attackers to exploit misconfigurations, access sensitive data, or gain control over cluster resources. Implementing Role-Based Access Control (RBAC) in Kubernetes is one of the most effective ways to enforce least privilege. RBAC defines fine-grained access policies based on roles, ensuring that users and applications only have access to the specific resources they need. Cluster administrators must create roles with minimal privileges and bind them to users, groups, and service accounts according to their operational requirements.

Service accounts in Kubernetes play a critical role in managing workload identities and interactions with the Kubernetes API. Many applications running in containers use service accounts to authenticate and communicate with cluster services. However, by default, Kubernetes assigns unnecessary permissions to service accounts, increasing the risk of privilege escalation. Implementing least privilege for service accounts involves restricting access using RBAC policies, disabling unnecessary API permissions, and using namespace-scoped service accounts instead of cluster-wide roles. Organizations should adopt a practice of explicitly defining service account roles rather than relying on default permissions, reducing the risk of unauthorized API access.

Pod Security Policies (PSP) or Pod Security Admission (PSA)

mechanisms enforce least privilege at the pod level by restricting capabilities, filesystem access, and privilege escalation settings. Containers often require elevated privileges to perform specific functions, but running pods with excessive capabilities increases security risks. Security best practices recommend using PSP or PSA policies to prevent privilege escalation by disallowing root user access, blocking privileged containers, and enforcing read-only filesystem configurations. Ensuring that containers run as non-root users reduces the risk of compromised workloads being exploited to gain higher-level access to the host system or Kubernetes cluster.

Network security is another critical aspect of least privilege in Kubernetes and containerized environments. Kubernetes uses network policies to control communication between pods, namespaces, and external services. Without proper network segmentation, attackers who gain access to a compromised container can laterally move within the cluster, increasing the risk of data breaches and service disruptions. Implementing least privilege in Kubernetes networking involves defining strict network policies that only allow necessary communication flows while blocking all unnecessary traffic. Using micro-segmentation, organizations can enforce granular network security policies to isolate workloads based on identity, role, and application dependencies.

Container runtime security plays a significant role in enforcing least privilege by restricting what containers can do within their execution environments. Attackers often exploit insecure container configurations, misconfigured privileges, or exposed container APIs to execute malicious actions. Applying least privilege at the container runtime level involves using security controls such as seccomp, AppArmor, and SELinux to restrict system calls, limit kernel interactions, and prevent unauthorized access to host resources. Ensuring that containers are built with minimal base images and removing unnecessary libraries and tools further reduces attack surfaces and eliminates potential security weaknesses.

Secrets management is essential to maintaining least privilege in

Kubernetes environments, as applications often require credentials, API tokens, and encryption keys to interact with cloud services and backend systems. Storing secrets in plaintext within container images, environment variables, or Kubernetes manifests increases the risk of credential exposure and unauthorized access. Kubernetes provides built-in secret management capabilities, but additional security best practices should be implemented, such as encrypting secrets at rest, using external secrets management solutions (e.g., HashiCorp Vault, AWS Secrets Manager, or Azure Key Vault), and enforcing least privilege access to secrets using RBAC policies.

Logging and monitoring enhance least privilege enforcement by providing visibility into security events, access attempts, and policy violations. Kubernetes-native monitoring tools, such as Prometheus, Fluentd, and OpenTelemetry, enable real-time detection of anomalous behaviors, failed access attempts, and unauthorized privilege escalations. Security Information and Event Management (SIEM) and User and Entity Behavior Analytics (UEBA) solutions further strengthen security by analyzing Kubernetes logs, detecting patterns of suspicious activity, and triggering automated security responses. By continuously monitoring container and cluster activity, organizations ensure that least privilege policies are enforced and potential security incidents are promptly addressed.

Compliance and regulatory requirements mandate strict access control policies, privilege management, and security monitoring for Kubernetes and containerized environments. Frameworks such as NIST 800-53, CIS Kubernetes Benchmarks, PCI DSS, and GDPR require organizations to implement least privilege access controls to protect sensitive data and prevent unauthorized system modifications. Enforcing compliance in Kubernetes involves auditing user roles, restricting administrative privileges, applying encryption for sensitive workloads, and generating audit logs for all access and authentication events. Automated compliance validation tools help organizations detect misconfigurations, enforce policy compliance, and reduce the risk of regulatory violations.

Privileged Access Management (PAM) extends least privilege enforcement by securing administrative access to Kubernetes clusters, containerized workloads, and cloud-native infrastructure. Cluster administrators and DevOps teams often require elevated permissions to deploy applications, modify configurations, and troubleshoot issues. However, granting persistent administrative access increases the risk of privilege abuse and insider threats. Implementing PAM solutions for Kubernetes ensures that privileged users authenticate using Multi-Factor Authentication (MFA), access management workflows, and just-in-time (JIT) privilege elevation. By applying least privilege principles to Kubernetes administration, organizations reduce the likelihood of privilege misuse and unauthorized system modifications.

Security automation enhances least privilege enforcement in Kubernetes by enabling continuous compliance checks, policy enforcement, and real-time threat mitigation. AI-driven security solutions analyze container behaviors, detect privilege escalation attempts, and automatically enforce security policies based on real-time risk assessments. Kubernetes-native security platforms, such as KubeArmor, Falco, and Aqua Security, provide automated policy enforcement, runtime threat detection, and least privilege enforcement for containerized applications. By integrating security automation with Kubernetes orchestration, organizations minimize human errors, improve response times, and maintain strong least privilege security postures.

Implementing least privilege in Kubernetes and containerized environments is essential for reducing attack surfaces, preventing unauthorized access, and ensuring compliance with security best practices. By enforcing RBAC policies, restricting network access, securing container runtimes, managing secrets properly, and leveraging security automation, organizations strengthen Kubernetes security while maintaining operational efficiency. As cloud-native architectures continue to evolve, least privilege remains a foundational principle for securing containerized workloads, protecting sensitive data, and mitigating emerging cyber threats in Kubernetes environments.

Zero Trust and Supply Chain Security

Zero Trust is a modern cybersecurity framework that assumes no entity—whether internal or external—should be inherently trusted. As supply chain attacks continue to rise, organizations must apply Zero Trust principles to secure their supply chains, ensuring that every component, partner, and vendor is continuously verified and monitored. Traditional security models often rely on perimeter-based defenses, assuming that trusted third parties and vendors operate securely. However, attackers frequently exploit weak links within supply chains, leveraging compromised software, hardware, or third-party access to infiltrate enterprise networks. By integrating Zero Trust with supply chain security, organizations enforce strict identity verification, least privilege access, and continuous monitoring to mitigate risks and prevent supply chain compromises.

Third-party risk management is a critical aspect of supply chain security. Organizations rely on suppliers, contractors, and service providers to maintain business operations, but these external entities often introduce security vulnerabilities. Attackers target suppliers with weak security controls, exploiting misconfigurations, stolen credentials, or malware-laden software updates to gain access to enterprise systems. Zero Trust enforces identity verification for third-party entities, requiring strong authentication mechanisms, such as multi-factor authentication (MFA), cryptographic certificates, and behavioral analytics, before granting access to enterprise resources. By continuously validating vendor credentials and monitoring their activities, organizations prevent unauthorized supply chain access and reduce the risk of compromised third parties introducing security threats.

Software supply chain security is another major concern, as attackers increasingly target software development pipelines to inject malicious code into trusted applications. Supply chain attacks, such as SolarWinds and Log4j, highlight the risks of compromised software dependencies and third-party libraries. Zero Trust mitigates these risks by enforcing strict code verification, ensuring that all software components are authenticated and signed before deployment. Software Bill of Materials (SBOM) provides transparency into software dependencies, enabling organizations to track and verify the origin of third-party code. By integrating Zero Trust with secure DevSecOps practices, organizations enforce continuous code validation, runtime security monitoring, and vulnerability scanning to detect and remediate software supply chain threats before they impact production environments.

Hardware supply chain security is equally critical, as attackers manipulate firmware, embedded systems, and device components to introduce backdoors, spyware, and unauthorized modifications. Many organizations source hardware from global suppliers, increasing the risk of counterfeit or tampered components entering enterprise networks. Zero Trust mandates strict vendor verification, requiring organizations to conduct thorough security assessments, implement cryptographic attestation for hardware components, and validate firmware integrity before deploying devices. Secure boot mechanisms, hardware-based encryption, and endpoint detection solutions further enhance supply chain security by preventing unauthorized modifications and ensuring that hardware components operate securely throughout their lifecycle.

Zero Trust Network Access (ZTNA) enhances supply chain security by replacing traditional VPN-based access models with identity-aware, context-driven access controls. Many supply chain attacks exploit excessive vendor permissions, allowing third-party users to move laterally across networks after initial authentication. ZTNA ensures that suppliers and contractors only access the specific applications and data they need, eliminating broad network access and reducing the risk of privilege escalation. If a vendor's security posture changes—such as logging in from an untrusted device or exhibiting anomalous behavior—ZTNA enforces additional authentication steps, session termination, or restricted access policies to prevent potential security breaches.

Identity governance and privileged access management (PAM) further strengthen Zero Trust supply chain security by enforcing least privilege access controls. Third-party administrators, contractors, and remote service providers often require elevated permissions to perform maintenance, troubleshoot systems, or update software. However, excessive privileges increase the risk of insider threats and credential abuse. Zero Trust enforces just-in-time (JIT) privileged access, ensuring that elevated permissions are granted only when necessary and revoked immediately after the task is completed. Continuous session monitoring and privileged activity logging ensure that all third-party access attempts are tracked, preventing unauthorized actions and enabling rapid response to security anomalies.

Continuous monitoring and real-time threat intelligence are essential to Zero Trust supply chain security, ensuring that potential threats are detected and mitigated before they escalate into breaches. Traditional security models rely on periodic audits and manual assessments, which fail to detect emerging risks in real time. Security Information and Event Management (SIEM) and User and Entity Behavior Analytics (UEBA) solutions integrate with Zero Trust frameworks to analyze third-party access patterns, detect suspicious behaviors, and trigger automated security responses. If a supplier suddenly accesses an unauthorized system, attempts to modify security configurations, or transfers large volumes of sensitive data, Zero Trust policies enforce immediate remediation actions, such as session isolation, access revocation, or security alerts for investigation.

Regulatory compliance mandates strict supply chain security controls, requiring organizations to enforce identity verification, access restrictions, and security monitoring for third-party interactions. Regulations such as GDPR, HIPAA, PCI DSS, NIST 800-161, and ISO 27001 emphasize supply chain risk management, ensuring that organizations validate supplier security practices, monitor third-party access, and implement secure software development processes. Zero Trust aligns with these compliance requirements by enforcing least privilege access, securing software delivery pipelines, and continuously assessing supply chain security risks. Automated compliance reporting ensures that organizations maintain regulatory adherence while reducing manual security assessments.

Cloud supply chain security presents additional challenges, as organizations increasingly rely on cloud service providers, SaaS applications, and third-party integrations to support business operations. Many cloud security incidents stem from misconfigured cloud permissions, exposed API keys, and insufficient vendor security controls. Zero Trust extends to cloud environments by enforcing identity-driven access policies, requiring encryption for cloud data transfers, and implementing continuous cloud security posture monitoring (CSPM). If a cloud vendor's security settings change or an API key is exposed, Zero Trust frameworks detect the anomaly and automatically enforce access restrictions to prevent potential compromise.

Artificial intelligence (AI) and automation enhance Zero Trust supply chain security by analyzing vendor risk profiles, detecting security anomalies, and enforcing real-time policy adjustments. AI-driven risk assessment tools continuously evaluate supplier security postures, flagging high-risk vendors and enforcing additional security requirements before granting access. Automated security workflows streamline third-party access reviews, ensuring that vendor permissions remain aligned with business needs and security policies. By integrating AI with Zero Trust supply chain security, organizations improve threat detection, accelerate incident response, and maintain proactive security measures against evolving supply chain threats.

Zero Trust provides a comprehensive security approach to protecting supply chains from cyber threats, ensuring that every vendor, software component, and hardware device is continuously verified and monitored. By enforcing least privilege access, integrating real-time threat intelligence, securing DevSecOps pipelines, and leveraging AI-driven automation, organizations mitigate supply chain risks while maintaining business continuity. As supply chain attacks grow in sophistication, adopting Zero Trust security frameworks remains essential for safeguarding enterprise ecosystems, preventing unauthorized access, and ensuring the integrity of software, hardware, and third-party relationships.

Using Blockchain for Identity and Access Management

Blockchain technology is transforming Identity and Access Management (IAM) by providing a decentralized, tamper-resistant, and transparent framework for identity verification, authentication, and authorization. Traditional IAM systems rely on centralized databases controlled by enterprises, governments, or identity providers, making them vulnerable to data breaches, identity theft, and single points of failure. Blockchain introduces a distributed ledger approach, ensuring that identity data is securely stored, cryptographically protected, and verifiable across multiple entities without requiring a central authority. By leveraging blockchain for IAM, organizations enhance security, reduce reliance on third-party intermediaries, and enable users to maintain greater control over their digital identities.

Decentralized identity, also known as self-sovereign identity (SSI), is a key application of blockchain in IAM. In traditional identity models, users must register with multiple service providers, creating numerous digital identities that require authentication through usernames, passwords, and third-party verification processes. This centralized approach increases the risk of credential compromise, identity fraud, and unauthorized access. Blockchain-based decentralized identity eliminates the need for intermediaries by allowing users to create, own, and control their identities using cryptographic keys. Instead of relying on centralized identity providers, users store their identity attributes on a blockchain ledger, granting access only to authorized entities when needed.

Smart contracts enhance blockchain-based IAM by automating identity verification and access control policies. Smart contracts are self-executing code stored on a blockchain that trigger predefined actions when specific conditions are met. In IAM, smart contracts enforce authentication rules, validate identity credentials, and authorize access to applications or resources without requiring manual intervention. For example, when a user attempts to access a cloud service, a smart contract can verify their blockchain-based credentials, check access permissions, and grant or deny access based on predefined policies. This reduces administrative overhead, minimizes human errors, and ensures consistent enforcement of security policies.

Public and private blockchains provide different approaches to IAM implementation. Public blockchains, such as Ethereum and Bitcoin, offer fully decentralized and transparent identity solutions, enabling users to manage their identities without relying on central authorities. However, public blockchains may not be suitable for enterprise IAM due to scalability concerns, high transaction costs, and data privacy regulations. Private and permissioned blockchains, such as Hyperledger Fabric and Corda, offer a more controlled environment, allowing organizations to manage IAM with restricted access, customizable security policies, and compliance-driven identity management. By selecting the appropriate blockchain model, organizations can balance decentralization, security, and regulatory compliance.

Zero Trust security frameworks integrate blockchain-based IAM to enforce continuous identity verification and least privilege access control. Unlike traditional perimeter-based security models that grant broad access after initial authentication, Zero Trust assumes that no entity should be inherently trusted. Blockchain enables continuous authentication by maintaining immutable identity records and verifying access requests in real-time. If a user's behavior deviates from normal patterns, Zero Trust policies can trigger reauthentication, require additional verification, or revoke access dynamically. This integration enhances identity security, reduces insider threats, and prevents credential-based attacks.

Multi-factor authentication (MFA) benefits from blockchain-based

IAM by eliminating reliance on centralized authentication servers. Traditional MFA solutions require users to authenticate using passwords, one-time passcodes, or biometric verification, often managed by third-party identity providers. Blockchain replaces these centralized mechanisms with cryptographic authentication, ensuring that MFA data remains secure and verifiable across decentralized networks. By leveraging blockchain for MFA, organizations reduce the risk of credential theft, phishing attacks, and authentication system compromise.

Access management in cloud environments is strengthened by blockchain-based IAM, ensuring secure and decentralized authentication for multi-cloud and hybrid IT infrastructures. Many organizations struggle with managing identities across different cloud providers, resulting in fragmented identity policies and increased security risks. Blockchain IAM provides a unified identity layer, allowing users to authenticate once and securely access cloud services across multiple platforms. Decentralized identity federation enables interoperability between cloud identity providers, reducing identity silos and simplifying access management for enterprises operating in complex cloud ecosystems.

Regulatory compliance mandates strict identity verification and access control requirements, making blockchain an attractive solution for securing sensitive data. Regulations such as GDPR, HIPAA, and PCI DSS emphasize data privacy, user consent, and secure identity management. Blockchain-based IAM ensures compliance by providing immutable audit trails, cryptographic data integrity, and user-controlled consent mechanisms. Organizations can leverage blockchain to store regulatory-compliant identity records, enforce access governance policies, and generate transparent audit logs for security assessments. By integrating blockchain with compliance frameworks, enterprises enhance data security while reducing regulatory risks.

Fraud prevention and identity theft mitigation are significant advantages of blockchain IAM, as decentralized identity systems eliminate the need for password-based authentication and reduce reliance on easily compromised credentials. Traditional IAM systems are prone to phishing attacks, credential stuffing, and database breaches, exposing user information to cybercriminals. Blockchain secures identity credentials using asymmetric cryptography, ensuring that authentication data remains confidential and tamper-proof. Even if an attacker compromises a user's device, they cannot manipulate blockchain-based identity records or impersonate the user without access to their private cryptographic keys.

Blockchain-based IAM enhances identity verification for Internet of Things (IoT) devices, ensuring secure authentication and access control in connected environments. IoT devices often lack robust identity management mechanisms, making them vulnerable to unauthorized access, botnet attacks, and device spoofing. Blockchain provides a decentralized trust model for IoT security, enabling device-to-device authentication, cryptographic identity verification, and tamper-resistant access control policies. By assigning each IoT device a unique blockchain identity, organizations prevent unauthorized devices from interacting with critical infrastructure and reduce the risk of IoT-driven cyber threats.

Artificial intelligence (AI) and automation further strengthen blockchain IAM by enabling real-time identity risk assessments, adaptive access policies, and automated identity verification processes. AI-driven analytics detect suspicious identity behaviors, unauthorized access attempts, and potential identity fraud in decentralized identity systems. By integrating AI with blockchain IAM, organizations enhance threat intelligence, dynamically adjust authentication policies, and automate security responses based on real-time identity risk analysis. AI-powered blockchain IAM reduces manual identity management efforts while improving security posture and user experience.

Organizations implementing blockchain for IAM must address scalability, interoperability, and adoption challenges. While blockchain provides enhanced security and decentralization, transaction speed and network latency remain concerns, especially for large-scale enterprise deployments. Hybrid blockchain architectures, sidechains, and off-chain identity verification mechanisms help mitigate these challenges, ensuring scalable and efficient blockchain IAM solutions. Additionally, interoperability between blockchain-based identity systems and traditional IAM frameworks is crucial for widespread adoption. Organizations must develop standardized identity protocols, integrate blockchain IAM with existing security infrastructures, and promote industry collaboration to accelerate blockchain IAM adoption.

Blockchain technology revolutionizes Identity and Access Management by providing a secure, decentralized, and transparent approach to identity verification, authentication, and access control. By leveraging decentralized identity, smart contracts, cryptographic authentication, and AI-driven security automation, organizations enhance IAM security while reducing reliance on centralized identity providers. As cyber threats continue to evolve, blockchain IAM remains a key innovation in protecting digital identities, securing cloud access, and mitigating identity-based attacks in modern enterprise environments.

User Experience vs. Security in Zero Trust IAM

Zero Trust Identity and Access Management (IAM) aims to eliminate implicit trust by enforcing continuous verification, least privilege access, and adaptive security controls. However, achieving strong security often comes at the expense of user experience, leading to frustration, reduced productivity, and potential workarounds that weaken security policies. Balancing user experience and security in Zero Trust IAM requires organizations to implement seamless authentication methods, adaptive access controls, and intelligent risk assessments that ensure robust protection without introducing unnecessary friction for legitimate users.

Traditional security models often rely on static authentication mechanisms, such as passwords, security questions, and periodic access reviews. These methods are susceptible to credential theft, phishing attacks, and human error, necessitating stricter authentication policies under Zero Trust. Multi-Factor Authentication (MFA) significantly enhances security by requiring additional verification factors, such as biometric authentication, one-time passcodes (OTP), or security tokens. However, frequent MFA prompts can disrupt user workflows, especially when users must reauthenticate multiple times throughout the day. Organizations must implement risk-based MFA, which dynamically adjusts authentication requirements based on user behavior, device trust, and contextual risk levels, reducing unnecessary authentication challenges while maintaining strong security.

Passwordless authentication improves both security and user experience by eliminating reliance on passwords, which are prone to phishing, brute-force attacks, and credential reuse. Traditional password policies often require complex, frequently changing credentials, leading to user frustration and increased support requests for password resets. Zero Trust IAM replaces passwords with more secure alternatives, such as biometric authentication, hardware security keys, and cryptographic authentication using FIDO2 and WebAuthn standards. These passwordless methods streamline authentication while reducing attack surfaces, enhancing both security and usability.

Single Sign-On (SSO) minimizes friction in Zero Trust environments by allowing users to authenticate once and gain access to multiple applications without repeatedly entering credentials. However, SSO must be carefully integrated with Zero Trust principles to prevent security gaps. Traditional SSO solutions often assume that authentication at the beginning of a session is sufficient, granting broad access for extended periods. Zero Trust IAM enforces continuous session validation, ensuring that user access is periodically reverified based on real-time security assessments. Implementing adaptive session expiration, step-up authentication, and behavioral analytics helps organizations maintain a secure SSO experience without disrupting user workflows.

Adaptive access controls leverage artificial intelligence and behavioral analytics to assess user risk dynamically, granting or restricting access based on contextual factors. Instead of enforcing static security policies for all users, Zero Trust IAM evaluates login behavior, device security posture, and historical access patterns to determine risk levels. If a user logs in from a familiar device and location, the system may allow seamless access without additional authentication. Conversely, if a user attempts to access sensitive data from an untrusted network or new device, Zero Trust policies can enforce step-up authentication, limit privileges, or require real-time identity verification. This approach maintains strong security while minimizing authentication friction for trusted users.

Context-aware security policies ensure that Zero Trust IAM adapts to different user scenarios without introducing unnecessary complexity. For example, employees working from corporate-managed devices may require fewer authentication challenges than those using personal or unmanaged endpoints. Organizations can implement conditional access policies that adjust security requirements based on endpoint compliance, location, and job function. By enforcing risk-based authentication dynamically, Zero Trust IAM maintains a seamless user experience while preventing unauthorized access from compromised or non-compliant devices.

Zero Trust IAM must also address the needs of privileged users and administrators, who require elevated access to critical systems while being prime targets for cyberattacks. Traditional security models often grant persistent privileged access, increasing the risk of insider threats and credential compromise. Zero Trust enforces just-in-time (JIT) privileged access, granting elevated permissions only when needed and revoking them immediately after use. While this approach strengthens security, it can introduce friction if not implemented effectively. Automating privilege escalation requests, integrating identity governance solutions, and using AI-driven risk assessments help streamline privileged access without slowing down critical administrative tasks.

User experience in Zero Trust IAM extends beyond authentication and access management to include seamless security workflows, self-service capabilities, and clear security communication. Many organizations struggle with security policies that disrupt workflows, forcing users to rely on IT support for access requests, password resets, and device enrollment. Implementing self-service identity verification, automated access reviews, and user-friendly security dashboards empowers employees while reducing administrative overhead. Providing clear, non-intrusive security notifications and guidance ensures that users understand security policies without feeling burdened by complex authentication requirements.

Integration with modern collaboration tools and cloud applications is essential for maintaining a positive user experience in Zero Trust IAM. Many enterprises use a mix of SaaS applications, remote work solutions, and hybrid IT environments, requiring seamless identity integration across multiple platforms. Federated identity solutions enable users to authenticate securely across different cloud providers without managing multiple sets of credentials. Identity orchestration platforms further enhance usability by connecting disparate IAM systems, ensuring a consistent authentication experience across various applications and services.

Regulatory compliance mandates strong identity security while ensuring accessibility and usability for employees, customers, and partners. Regulations such as GDPR, HIPAA, and PCI DSS require organizations to enforce strict identity verification and access control measures while maintaining user-friendly security processes. Zero Trust IAM solutions must align with compliance requirements by implementing audit logging, automated access certifications, and user activity monitoring. Ensuring that compliance measures do not introduce excessive friction requires organizations to adopt intelligent security automation, reducing manual interventions while maintaining regulatory adherence.

Security culture plays a critical role in balancing Zero Trust IAM security with user experience. Employees often perceive security policies as obstacles rather than enablers of secure access. Organizations must foster a security-first mindset by educating users on the importance of Zero Trust principles, demonstrating how adaptive authentication enhances security without hindering productivity. Providing security training, gamification, and real-world attack simulations helps users understand threats such as phishing, social engineering, and credential theft, reinforcing secure behaviors while maintaining engagement.

Artificial intelligence and machine learning enhance Zero Trust IAM by continuously optimizing authentication experiences and access policies based on real-time risk analysis. AI-driven identity analytics detect suspicious behavior, adapt security policies dynamically, and automate identity verification workflows. By leveraging AI for behavioral biometrics, anomaly detection, and continuous authentication, Zero Trust IAM improves security while reducing authentication friction for legitimate users. AI-driven automation ensures that access controls remain fluid, adjusting to evolving threats and user behaviors without introducing unnecessary complexity.

Organizations must strike a balance between strong security and user experience in Zero Trust IAM to ensure seamless authentication, secure access control, and minimal disruption to workflows. By adopting risk-based authentication, passwordless security, adaptive access controls, and AI-driven automation, enterprises enhance identity protection while maintaining usability. As Zero Trust adoption continues to grow, organizations must prioritize user experience alongside security, ensuring that identity verification remains robust, frictionless, and adaptive to modern workforce needs.

Zero Trust IAM Case Studies and Real-World Implementations

Zero Trust Identity and Access Management (IAM) has been widely adopted across various industries to enhance security, minimize insider threats, and prevent unauthorized access. Organizations transitioning from traditional perimeter-based security models to Zero Trust IAM have experienced significant improvements in risk management, compliance, and operational efficiency. Real-world implementations highlight how companies across different sectors apply Zero Trust IAM principles to secure access, enforce least privilege, and protect sensitive data from cyber threats.

A major financial institution implemented Zero Trust IAM to address the growing threat of credential-based attacks and unauthorized access to banking systems. The organization had previously relied on role-based access control (RBAC) and virtual private networks (VPNs) to secure remote access for employees and third-party vendors. However, a security audit revealed excessive user privileges, dormant accounts with access to critical systems, and phishing attacks that exploited weak authentication mechanisms. The financial institution adopted Zero Trust IAM by enforcing adaptive multi-factor authentication (MFA), eliminating VPNs in favor of Zero Trust Network Access (ZTNA), and implementing continuous monitoring of user activity. With AI-driven behavioral analytics, the organization reduced unauthorized access incidents by 80%, ensuring that employees and vendors could only access financial systems based on real-time risk assessments.

A multinational healthcare provider faced compliance challenges related to HIPAA regulations and patient data security. Traditional IAM policies granted broad access to electronic health records (EHRs) for doctors, nurses, and administrative staff, increasing the risk of insider threats and accidental data exposure. The provider implemented Zero Trust IAM by integrating identity-based micro-segmentation, just-in-time (JIT) privileged access, and biometric authentication for high-risk transactions. Access to EHRs was restricted based on job roles, location, and device security posture, ensuring that healthcare professionals could only retrieve patient records relevant to their responsibilities. Automated identity governance and continuous access evaluations helped the provider maintain regulatory compliance while reducing the risk of data breaches.

A leading technology company operating in a multi-cloud environment faced challenges managing identities across multiple cloud platforms, including AWS, Azure, and Google Cloud. The company experienced difficulty enforcing consistent access policies, monitoring privileged access, and securing API credentials. By deploying a Zero Trust IAM framework, the organization implemented federated identity management, passwordless authentication, and API security policies to prevent unauthorized access. Identity threat detection and response (ITDR) solutions continuously monitored cloud access patterns, detecting anomalies and automatically revoking access when suspicious activity was identified. The implementation led to a 60% reduction in cloud-based security incidents and improved operational efficiency by eliminating the need for multiple identity management systems.

A global manufacturing company with an extensive supply chain ecosystem struggled with securing third-party vendor access to internal systems. Many suppliers required access to procurement portals, logistics data, and IoT-connected manufacturing equipment, but traditional VPN-based security models exposed the company to significant risks. Zero Trust IAM was implemented by enforcing vendor identity proofing, just-in-time access provisioning, and continuous session validation. Zero Trust Network Access (ZTNA) replaced VPNs, ensuring that vendors only accessed approved applications without gaining broader network privileges. AI-powered identity analytics detected potential third-party security risks, reducing supply chain attack attempts by 70% and improving overall supply chain security.

A government agency responsible for national cybersecurity initiatives adopted Zero Trust IAM to protect sensitive intelligence data and critical infrastructure systems. The agency transitioned from perimeter-based security models to a Zero Trust architecture that enforced strict identity verification, continuous authentication, and privilege escalation monitoring. Role-based and attribute-based access controls (RBAC/ABAC) ensured that users accessed information based on security clearance levels and real-time risk assessments. Identity governance solutions enforced strict audit logging and compliance monitoring, helping the agency meet regulatory requirements while strengthening national security. The shift to Zero Trust IAM prevented several attempted nation-state cyberattacks and ensured the confidentiality of classified data.

A major e-commerce platform implemented Zero Trust IAM to combat fraud, account takeovers, and unauthorized financial transactions. The company integrated AI-driven identity verification, adaptive authentication, and risk-based transaction monitoring to secure customer and employee accounts. Behavioral analytics detected anomalies in login attempts, payment processing, and account modifications, triggering additional authentication steps when suspicious behavior was identified. By applying Zero Trust principles, the platform reduced fraudulent transactions by 50% and enhanced customer trust in the security of their personal and financial information.

An international airline faced challenges securing its workforce, frequent travelers, and airport operations due to the complexity of managing identities across multiple locations. Employees, contractors, and airport staff required access to different systems, from flight scheduling to baggage handling and customer service applications. Zero Trust IAM was implemented to enforce identity-based segmentation, requiring continuous authentication for high-risk transactions such as flight crew scheduling and aircraft maintenance approvals. Secure biometric authentication replaced traditional password-based logins, streamlining airport security while reducing identity-related fraud. By adopting Zero Trust IAM, the airline improved workforce security, minimized insider threats, and reduced unauthorized access incidents by 65%.

A large retail organization with a hybrid IT environment transitioned to Zero Trust IAM to secure employee access to point-of-sale (POS) systems, inventory management platforms, and customer data. Many retail employees used shared workstations and mobile devices, increasing the risk of credential theft and unauthorized system access. Zero Trust IAM policies enforced step-up authentication for high-value transactions, ensuring that employees authenticated using secure tokens or biometrics before processing sensitive customer information. AI-driven fraud detection identified suspicious employee activities, preventing internal fraud and unauthorized data exfiltration. The implementation improved security across 2,000 retail locations while maintaining a seamless customer experience.

An energy company responsible for managing critical infrastructure, including power grids and oil refineries, adopted Zero Trust IAM to protect against cyberattacks targeting operational technology (OT) environments. Traditional IAM policies lacked granular access controls for OT systems, increasing the risk of cyber-physical attacks. Zero Trust IAM introduced least privilege access policies, network segmentation, and continuous security monitoring for industrial control systems (ICS). By enforcing strict access governance and integrating IAM with threat detection platforms, the company prevented several cyber intrusion attempts while ensuring the availability and security of critical energy infrastructure.

Zero Trust IAM implementations across various industries demonstrate the effectiveness of identity-driven security strategies in reducing cyber risks, preventing unauthorized access, and ensuring compliance with regulatory frameworks. Organizations that successfully transition to Zero Trust IAM leverage adaptive authentication, behavioral analytics, and automated identity governance to enhance security while maintaining operational efficiency. By adopting real-time risk assessments and continuous identity validation, businesses, governments, and service providers strengthen their security postures against evolving threats and ensure that only verified, authorized users access sensitive systems and data.

Zero Trust IAM Maturity Models and Roadmaps

Zero Trust Identity and Access Management (IAM) is not a one-time implementation but an evolving strategy that organizations must mature over time. The journey from traditional perimeter-based security to a fully mature Zero Trust IAM framework requires structured planning, continuous improvement, and phased implementation. Maturity models provide organizations with a structured way to assess their current Zero Trust IAM capabilities, identify gaps, and develop roadmaps for achieving higher levels of identity security. A well-defined Zero Trust IAM roadmap ensures that security measures align with business goals while minimizing disruptions to operations.

Organizations typically progress through multiple stages in their Zero Trust IAM maturity journey. The initial stage, often referred to as the traditional or reactive phase, relies heavily on legacy identity management practices. Access control mechanisms are static, authentication is primarily password-based, and user provisioning lacks automation. Many organizations at this stage struggle with excessive privileges, lack of visibility into identity-related risks, and limited enforcement of least privilege principles. Security teams often rely on network-based trust models, assuming that users and devices inside the corporate network are inherently trusted. This outdated approach leaves organizations vulnerable to credential theft, insider threats, and lateral movement attacks.

The next stage in the Zero Trust IAM maturity model involves moving toward an identity-centric security approach. Organizations begin implementing Multi-Factor Authentication (MFA) to reduce reliance on passwords and enhance user verification. Role-Based Access Control (RBAC) is introduced to enforce least privilege, ensuring that users only have access to the resources necessary for their job functions. Identity lifecycle management improves through automation, reducing the risk of orphaned accounts and privilege creep. At this stage, organizations start integrating Identity Governance and Administration (IGA) solutions to enforce access reviews, track privileged user activities, and align identity security with compliance requirements.

As organizations advance in their Zero Trust IAM maturity, they adopt adaptive authentication and risk-based access control mechanisms. Instead of relying on static authentication rules, access policies become dynamic, adjusting in real time based on contextual risk factors such as user behavior, device trust, and location. Zero Trust Network Access (ZTNA) replaces traditional VPNs, restricting access to applications based on identity verification rather than network-based trust. Privileged Access Management (PAM) is fully integrated, ensuring that administrative users receive just-in-time (JIT) access rather than persistent privileges. Machine identities, including service accounts and API keys, are secured with strong authentication and lifecycle management controls.

At the highest level of Zero Trust IAM maturity, organizations achieve full automation, continuous monitoring, and AI-driven threat detection for identity-related risks. Identity and User Behavior Analytics (UEBA) are integrated with IAM systems, providing continuous risk assessments and anomaly detection. Artificial intelligence (AI) and machine learning enhance security decision-making by identifying suspicious access patterns, automating threat response actions, and dynamically adjusting identity policies based on evolving risk conditions. Compliance is streamlined through automated audit reporting, ensuring that security controls align with regulatory requirements such as GDPR, HIPAA, and NIST 800-53. Organizations at this stage enforce Zero Trust principles across all identity types, including human users, machine identities, IoT devices, and cloud workloads.

Developing a roadmap for Zero Trust IAM implementation requires organizations to assess their current maturity level and establish clear objectives for each phase of their transformation. The first step in the roadmap is conducting a security assessment to identify identity-related vulnerabilities, excessive permissions, and authentication weaknesses. Organizations should prioritize high-risk areas, such as privileged accounts, third-party access, and cloud identity security. Based on this assessment, security teams can define key milestones, allocate resources, and establish a governance structure for Zero Trust IAM adoption.

The next phase of the roadmap focuses on strengthening authentication and access control mechanisms. Organizations should transition from password-based authentication to MFA, ensuring that all users—employees, contractors, and partners—verify their identities using multiple factors. Risk-based authentication should be introduced to reduce friction for low-risk users while enforcing additional verification for high-risk access attempts. Identity federation and Single Sign-On (SSO) enable seamless authentication across enterprise applications, improving user experience while maintaining security.

As organizations progress, the roadmap should include enhancements in least privilege enforcement and identity governance. Implementing Role-Based Access Control (RBAC) and Attribute-Based Access Control (ABAC) ensures that users, applications, and systems have only the permissions necessary to perform their tasks. Access policies should be continuously reviewed and adjusted based on real-time risk assessments, preventing privilege escalation and insider threats. Organizations should integrate identity lifecycle automation, ensuring that access is granted, modified, and revoked based on business needs rather than manual approvals.

To further strengthen Zero Trust IAM maturity, organizations should integrate continuous monitoring and real-time threat detection. Security teams should deploy UEBA solutions to analyze identity behaviors, detect anomalies, and prevent unauthorized access attempts. Security Information and Event Management (SIEM) and automated response mechanisms should be configured to detect identity-based threats and enforce remediation actions. By integrating identity security with endpoint security, network segmentation, and cloud access controls, organizations ensure that Zero Trust IAM is embedded into the broader security architecture.

A fully mature Zero Trust IAM framework also requires organizations to extend security controls to third-party identities and non-human entities. Many security breaches originate from compromised vendor credentials, weak supply chain security, and misconfigured API access. Organizations should enforce third-party identity proofing, require strong authentication for external users, and implement Zero Trust Network Access (ZTNA) for suppliers and contractors. Machine identity management should be strengthened by rotating API keys, securing service accounts, and enforcing strict access policies for cloud-based workloads.

The final stage in the Zero Trust IAM roadmap involves continuous optimization, automation, and AI-driven identity security enhancements. Organizations should implement AI-powered identity analytics to predict and prevent identity-based threats proactively. Automated policy enforcement ensures that identity security controls remain effective, adapting to changes in user roles, business operations, and threat landscapes. Organizations should also conduct regular Zero Trust IAM audits, measuring the effectiveness of security controls and adjusting strategies based on emerging risks. By continuously refining identity security practices, organizations maintain resilience against evolving cyber threats while enabling secure and efficient access for users.

Zero Trust IAM maturity models and roadmaps provide organizations with a structured approach to transitioning from traditional identity security to a fully automated and risk-aware IAM framework. By adopting a phased implementation strategy, organizations gradually strengthen authentication mechanisms, enforce least privilege access, integrate AI-driven analytics, and align IAM security with Zero Trust principles. As cyber threats continue to evolve, achieving Zero Trust IAM maturity ensures that organizations remain agile, secure, and compliant in an increasingly complex digital landscape.

Conclusion: The Path Forward for Zero Trust and Least Privilege in IAM

Zero Trust and least privilege in Identity and Access Management (IAM) represent the future of cybersecurity, providing organizations with a resilient framework to mitigate identity-based threats, prevent unauthorized access, and enforce continuous authentication. As cyber threats evolve and organizations expand their digital ecosystems, the importance of identity security grows, requiring a proactive and adaptive approach. The journey toward a fully mature Zero Trust IAM framework is ongoing, demanding continuous assessment, technology integration, and policy refinement to ensure robust security while maintaining usability for employees, partners, and customers.

Organizations adopting Zero Trust IAM must recognize that security is no longer about securing a traditional network perimeter but rather about protecting identities, data, and applications regardless of their location. Legacy security models that assume implicit trust within corporate networks have proven ineffective in the face of sophisticated cyberattacks, insider threats, and supply chain compromises. The modern workforce operates across hybrid cloud environments, remote work setups, and decentralized digital ecosystems, making Zero Trust IAM a necessity rather than an option. By enforcing strict identity verification, continuous authentication, and least privilege access controls, organizations eliminate the risks associated with excessive trust and static access policies.

The adoption of Zero Trust IAM requires a strategic approach that balances security with user experience. Excessive security measures can create friction, leading to productivity losses and user frustration, while overly permissive policies increase the risk of unauthorized access. Organizations must implement risk-based authentication, adaptive access controls, and AI-driven identity analytics to ensure that security measures are dynamically adjusted based on user behavior, device trust, and contextual risk factors. Passwordless authentication, biometric verification, and single sign-on (SSO) solutions help streamline authentication processes while reducing reliance on vulnerable credential-based access methods.

As Zero Trust IAM continues to evolve, automation and artificial intelligence will play an increasingly critical role in identity security. AI-driven identity threat detection and response (ITDR) solutions enhance traditional IAM frameworks by providing real-time anomaly detection, continuous risk assessments, and automated policy enforcement. Machine learning models analyze access patterns, detect privilege escalation attempts, and enforce least privilege dynamically, reducing the likelihood of credential misuse and insider threats. By integrating AI into IAM, organizations strengthen identity security while minimizing the need for manual oversight and administrative intervention.

Regulatory compliance and governance will remain key drivers for Zero Trust IAM adoption. Organizations operating in highly regulated industries such as healthcare, finance, and government must ensure compliance with standards such as GDPR, HIPAA, PCI DSS, and NIST 800-53. Zero Trust IAM frameworks align with regulatory requirements by enforcing strict identity verification, access governance, and audit logging. Automated compliance monitoring solutions simplify adherence to these regulations, reducing the complexity of manual security audits while ensuring that access policies remain consistent with industry best practices.

Securing non-human identities is an emerging priority in Zero Trust IAM. As organizations increasingly rely on cloud services, DevOps workflows, and API-driven integrations, managing machine identities becomes as important as securing human users. Many cyberattacks exploit misconfigured service accounts, exposed API keys, and excessive permissions granted to automated processes. Zero Trust IAM extends least privilege principles to machine identities, ensuring that non-human entities authenticate using strong cryptographic methods, operate with minimal access permissions, and are continuously monitored for anomalous activity.

Zero Trust IAM also plays a crucial role in supply chain security, preventing cyberattacks that target third-party vendors, contractors, and service providers. Supply chain compromises, such as software supply chain attacks and third-party credential theft, have become significant security risks for organizations worldwide. Zero Trust IAM enforces strict third-party identity verification, just-in-time access provisioning, and continuous session validation to prevent unauthorized supply chain access. By integrating identity-based micro-segmentation and Zero Trust Network Access (ZTNA), organizations minimize the risk of supply chain attacks while enabling secure collaboration with external partners.

As organizations expand their digital infrastructures, implementing Zero Trust IAM in cloud environments remains a critical priority. Cloud identity security challenges, including misconfigured access controls, excessive permissions, and unprotected API endpoints, expose organizations to identity-based cyber threats. Multi-cloud IAM strategies ensure that Zero Trust policies are enforced consistently across cloud platforms such as AWS, Azure, and Google Cloud. Federated identity management, cloud-native access controls, and Zero Trust cloud security architectures provide seamless identity protection across hybrid environments, reducing the risks associated with fragmented IAM implementations.

The integration of Zero Trust IAM with endpoint security strengthens identity protection by ensuring that users access corporate resources only from secure and compliant devices. Many cyberattacks exploit vulnerabilities in unmanaged endpoints, leveraging stolen credentials to gain unauthorized access to enterprise systems. Zero Trust IAM enforces device health checks, endpoint security posture assessments, and conditional access policies that restrict access from compromised or non-compliant devices. By aligning identity security with endpoint protection, organizations create a unified security framework that prevents credential-based attacks and unauthorized lateral movement within corporate networks.

Future advancements in Zero Trust IAM will focus on decentralization and blockchain-based identity management. Traditional IAM models rely on centralized identity providers, creating single points of failure and increasing the risk of large-scale identity breaches. Decentralized identity (DID) solutions, powered by blockchain technology, enable users to maintain control over their digital identities while ensuring tamper-proof authentication and access verification. Self-sovereign identity (SSI) frameworks reduce reliance on third-party identity providers, allowing users to authenticate securely without exposing personal credentials to centralized databases. As decentralized identity solutions gain traction, Zero Trust IAM frameworks will evolve to incorporate blockchain-based authentication, reducing identity-related security risks.

Continuous IAM maturity assessments and strategic roadmaps ensure that organizations sustain long-term Zero Trust adoption. The journey to Zero Trust IAM is not a single implementation but a continuous evolution that requires iterative improvements, regular security assessments, and alignment with emerging threats and technologies. Organizations must establish IAM maturity models that evaluate current security capabilities, identify areas for enhancement, and develop phased roadmaps for achieving Zero Trust IAM excellence. Regular security training, user awareness programs, and stakeholder engagement further reinforce the adoption of Zero Trust principles across enterprise environments.

By embracing Zero Trust IAM, organizations future-proof their identity security strategies against evolving cyber threats, ensuring that access control remains dynamic, risk-aware, and continuously verified. Implementing least privilege access, integrating AI-driven security intelligence, and adopting decentralized identity solutions enable organizations to build a resilient IAM framework that enhances security while maintaining operational efficiency. The future of Zero Trust IAM lies in continuous innovation, strategic adaptation, and a relentless commitment to securing identities across digital ecosystems.